FISHERMEN'S SWEATERS

FISHERMEN'S SWEATERS

20 EXCLUSIVE KNITWEAR DESIGNS FOR ALL GENERATIONS

ALICE STARMORE

Trafalgar Square Publishing

NORTH POMFRET, VERMONT

To the memory of Annie Macleod, 1912–1930

First published in the United States of America in 1993 by
Trafalgar Square Publishing, North Pomfret, Vermont 05053

First published in Great Britain in 1993 by
Anaya Publishers Ltd, London

Editor Sally Harding
Designer Clare Clements
Photographer Mike Bunn
Stylist Karen Harrison
Pattern Checker Marilyn Wilson
Charts and Measurement Diagrams Windfall Press
Knitting Techniques Illustrator Coral Mula

Library of Congress Catalog Card Number: 93-60141

ISBN 0-943955-73-4

Typeset in Great Britain by Textype Typesetters, Cambridge
Colour reproduction by J. Film Process, Singapore
Printed and bound in China

CONTENTS

INTRODUCTION

Of all the different knitting traditions in the world, the technique of knitting fisher ganseys entirely in the round is the most technically and visually sophisticated. This is my opinion, and my claims to lack of bias will probably not be believed. I was born and brought up in a Scottish fishing community where ganseys were avidly knitted, and I learned to knit them myself in much the same way as I learned to talk. My knitting roots are firmly established in this area. As a professional designer, however, I constantly use and have written about most other traditional techniques; but nothing satisfies my eye for detail and my appreciation of knitting mathematics and expert construction, like a well-executed gansey, knitted in the round.

The technique was born of sheer practicality – for the warmth and comfort of men pursuing a hard life at sea. It was practised by equally hard-working, largely unlettered women, who combined this practicality with decorative and aesthetic elements to produce garments that, at their best, belong to the realm of wearable art. It may seem strange, then, that in Britain – where the most sophisticated and elaborate ganseys were produced – this form of knitting is now almost extinct. The aims of this book are clear and simple: to revive interest in the technique, to celebrate its achievements and to carry it forward with new developments.

Why is the technique now virtually unpractised? Knitting sweaters entirely in the round is not difficult. It does, however, require a certain amount of practice and diligence. Furthermore, designers with the ability to write patterns for authentic ganseys are very thin on the ground. When knitted sweaters became fashionable in the 1920's yarn companies and women's magazines began to publish patterns. The designers of those patterns approached knitting from a dressmaking basis and were not traditional knitters. As I have mentioned, the true technique lay in the hands of unlettered women, and no-one outside the fishing communities made any attempt to master it. It was much easier to write instructions for flat pieces to be sewn together than to master the intricacies of the authentic method.

Some early attempts were made to publish instructions for simple ganseys, but they were very vague and both technique and design were corrupted. Take the sleeves, for example. In some instructions, the sleeves – although knitted in the round – were to be knitted separately and then grafted on around the armholes. This compromise method was not used by skilled gansey knitters. It is clumsy and defeats an important practical purpose. The gansey sleeve should be knitted by picking up around the armhole and working to the cuff. This means that the cuffs and elbows – which in a working man's sweater always wear out first – can be easily replaced by unravelling to the elbow and re-knitting. This is why so many past ganseys featured sleeves that were patterned to the elbow and then worked plain to the cuff. Though the aim was practical the result also provided a very positive design feature, as you can see in my child's design *Fife* (page 29).

Any knitter who has made a gansey in the original circular technique can immediately see the practical advantages of the method, and it is also easy to see how the technique enables all the design details to emerge. I feel avery strongly that this traditional method of construction should be revived for knitters today, and so thirteen out of the twenty designs in this book are knitted in the circular technique. As well as providing detailed instructions for each sweater, I have included a comprehensive guide for circular knitting in the technical chapter for those of you who have never tried this before. The stamp of a real gansey is its detail – its underarm and neck gussets, its shoulder straps and its intricate arrangement of patterns. In designing this collection, I have sought to give a thorough exposition of all these authentic touches.

I have structured my twenty original designs in the form of an imaginary voyage, stopping off at various ports of call. It was natural to start in Scotland, specifically in my home town of Stornoway. The women in my family, in common with most Scottish gansey knitters, knitted for the male members of their families, and the hallmark of their knitting was elaborate individuality. Each garment would be designed (this was never done on paper) for an individual size and would therefore require stitch patterns that fit exactly. A lot of creative activity went on, resulting in friendly and lively competition between knitters, and great pride on the part of any wearer who was lucky enough to have the best. In a community of expert knitters, there was occasionally someone who had that extra spark of creativity and talent. These women, now dead, are still remembered and spoken of with admiration.

Although many English knitters also designed for their own families, a great deal of contract knitting went on. This is manifest in their plainer ganseys which were faster to knit and made for sale. English gansey style and pattern were pared down to their essence, and when well executed, these knitted garments had a simple elegance of their own. My design *Cornwall* (page 36) is closely based on this idea.

The Irish knitters from Aran knitted ganseys in the Scottish style until they developed their own famed Aran sweaters around the 1930's. These were based on complex cabled forms and worked in a heavy yarn. By this time the flat knitting technique was well established, and in this case was more practical to use, as the yarn was so heavy that a one piece garment would be very unwieldly to work on.

A call at various regions in Northern Europe and the continent allowed me to introduce some colour to the book. Adapting the essence of styles in each particular area, I designed four sweaters for this chapter.

This metaphorical journey concludes in the New World. My aim here was to create designs that take a fresh look at the tradition of fishermen's sweaters and that take my favourite features in new directions. I consequently named these designs after North American ports of call. They have some entirely new stitch patterns that I designed specially; they have old

stitch patterns put together in new ways; and they feature some fresh details, such as patterned gussets (see page 109 for a picture of a patterned gusset).

There is also a personal reason for ending the voyage in the New World. My aunt, Annie Macleod, was one of those individuals in whom the creative spark was particularly strong. She was fascinated with the idea of North America and longed to go there. In 1930 – at the age of eighteen – she left her native Isle of Lewis on an emigrant ship bound for Canada. My mother vividly remembers the entire wardrobe of clothes that she made for the voyage and her new life. While at sea she contracted meningitis and died on arrival in Quebec. This book is dedicated to her memory.

The sharp lines of Inishmore *are in subtle contrast with the more rounded shape of the twisted-rib cable and the smooth texture of the branched cable (above). The zigzag panels extend into the saddle shoulders (see page 56).*

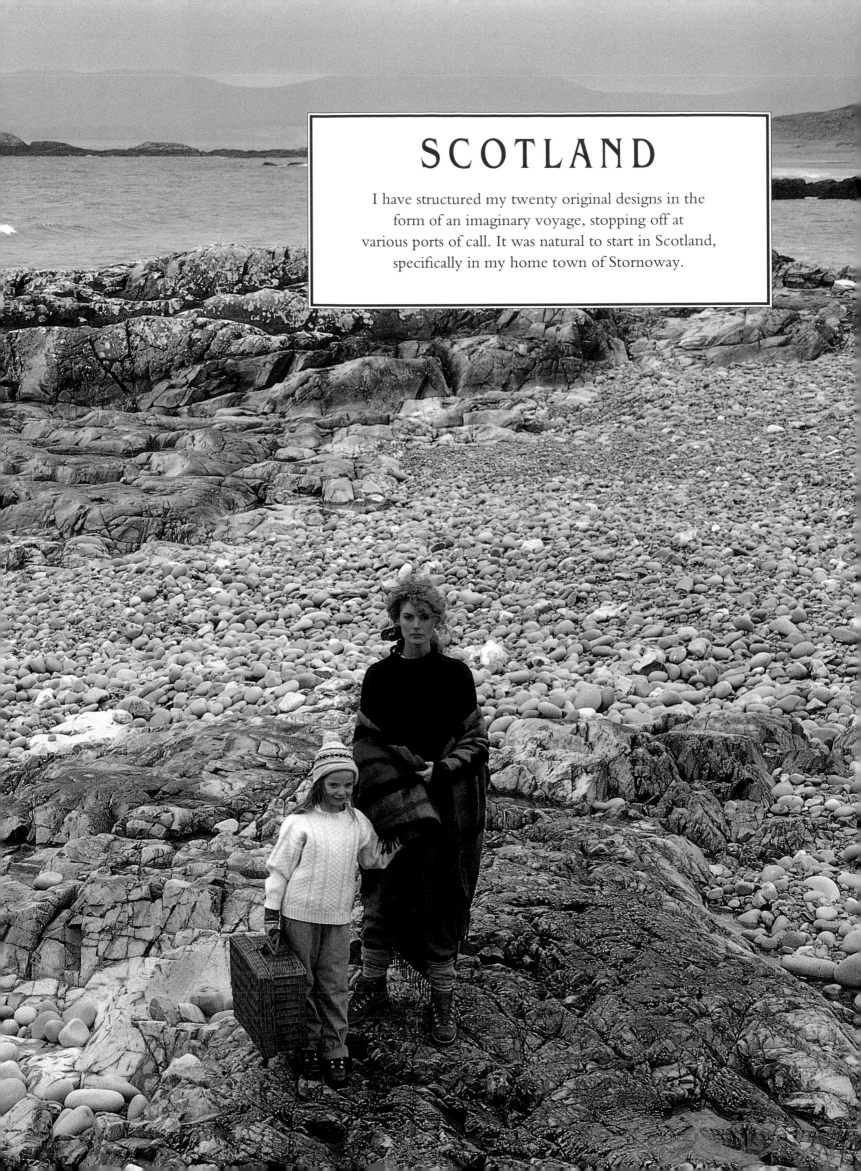

SCOTLAND

I have structured my twenty original designs in the
form of an imaginary voyage, stopping off at
various ports of call. It was natural to start in Scotland,
specifically in my home town of Stornoway.

STORNOWAY

SIZES

To fit medium [large, extra large]
Directions for larger sizes are given in brackets. Where there is only one set of figures, it applies to all sizes.

KNITTED MEASUREMENTS

Underarm, excluding gussets 113[121, 128]cm (45[48,51]in)
Length 65[67.5,70]cm (25½[26½,27½]in)
Sleeve length 46[48,51]cm (18¼[19,20]in)

MATERIALS

Yarn weight used: 5-ply gansey wool (US sport)
11[12,13] x 100g (3½oz) balls of Alice Starmore's *Scottish Fleet* in Navy
1 set of double-pointed *or* circular 2¾mm (US 2) and 3mm (US 3) needles
1 cable needle
8 stitch holders
Stitch markers

TENSION (GAUGE)

15 sts and 19 rows to 5cm (2in) measured over st st, using 3mm (US 3) needles (see note below)

SPECIAL NOTE

The sweater is entirely patterned throughout. The st st tension (gauge) swatch simply makes it easier to accurately measure the tension (gauge).

BODY

Body is worked in one piece to armhole.
With 2¾mm (US 2) needles, cast on 316[336,356] sts.
Place a st marker on RH needle to mark beg of rnd, then making sure cast-on edge is not twisted and working in rnds (RS always facing), work k2, p2 rib for 7[7.5,7.5]cm (2¾[3,3]in), slipping marker on each rnd.
Inc rnd: (M1, k4) 19 times; (m1, k5) 2[4,6] times; (m1, k4) 37 times; (m1, k5) 2[4,6] times; (m1, k4) 18 times.
394[418,442] sts.
Change to 3mm (US 3) needles and

*M*y earliest memories of observing fisher ganseys in everyday working use are at the harbour town of Stornoway, where I was born. I feel it is therefore appropriate that I should begin with Stornoway, which is based on the working gansey and the types of patterns and techniques that typify the Scottish tradition. The result is a rugged and masculine design, which is reflected by its generous sizing.

reading charts from right to left and beg all charts from rnd 1, set patt as follows—
Chart rnd 1: Keeping marker in place to mark first st for beg of rnd and underarm seam st, ★★k seam st; work chart A for relevant size over next 21[23,25] sts; work chart B over next 14 sts; work chart C for relevant size over next 21[23,25] sts; ★work chart B over next 14 sts; work chart D for relevant size over next 21[23,25] sts★; rep from ★ to ★ once; work chart B over next 14 sts; work chart

Cover next 21[23,25] sts; work chart B over next 14 sts; work chart A over next 21[23,25] sts★★; place a st marker on RH needle to mark next st for centre of rnd and underarm seam st, then rep from ★★ to ★★ once more.
Reading every chart rnd from right to left, cont in chart patts as set, rep all rnds of each chart until body measures 31[32.5,33]cm (12¼[12¾,13]in) from cast-on edge, slipping markers on every rnd throughout and ending after working an even number of chart patt rnds.
Begin Gussets
Next rnd: M1; k seam st; m1; keeping continuity, work in patt as set to next underarm seam st; m1; k seam st; m1; keeping continuity of patt, work in patt to end of rnd. (The seam st and the inc sts form the gussets – there are now 3 sts in each gusset.)
Cont working chart patts as set over back and front sts and working all gusset sts in st st throughout, inc 1 st at each side of each gusset on every foll 4th rnd until there are 19[21,23] sts in each gusset. 430[458,486] sts.
Divide for Yokes
Place first 19[21,23] sts of rnd (gusset) on a holder, leave next 196[208,220] sts (back yoke sts) on a spare needle, place next 19[21,23] sts (gusset) on a holder. 196[208,220] sts of front yoke rem.
Front Yoke
Beg with a WS row and keeping continuity, work 196[208,220] sts of front yoke back and forth in rows (now reading WS chart rows from left to right and RS rows from right to left) until yoke measures 18cm (7in) from top of gussets, ending with RS facing for next row.
Shape Front Neck
Next row (RS): Keeping continuity, work 74[79,84] sts in patt; place next 48[50,52] sts on a holder; turn, leaving rem sts on a spare needle.
Keeping continuity of patt as far as possible, shape left side of neck as follows—
Dec 1 st at neck edge on next and every foll alt row until 65[69,73] sts rem, so ending with RS facing for next row.

FIRST SIZE, CHART A

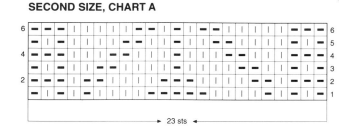

21 sts

SECOND SIZE, CHART A

23 sts

FIRST SIZE, CHART C

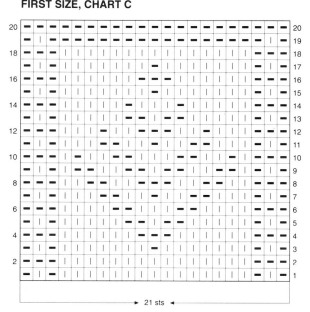

21 sts

SECOND SIZE, CHART C

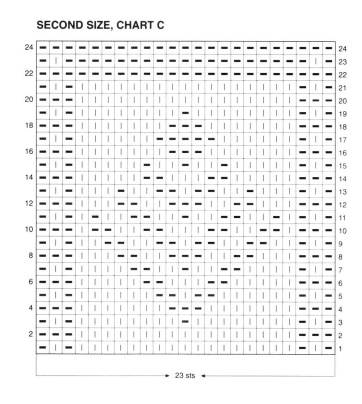

23 sts

FIRST SIZE, CHART D

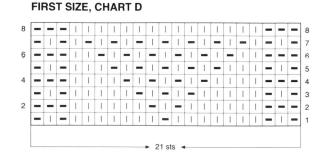

21 sts

SECOND SIZE, CHART D

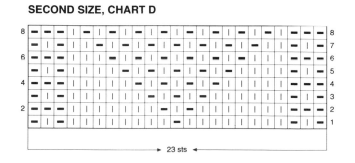

23 sts

THIRD SIZE, CHART A

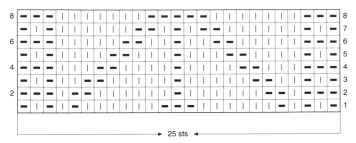

→ 25 sts ←

ALL SIZES, CHART B

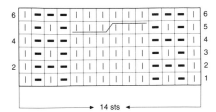

→ 14 sts ←

KEY

□	k on RS rows; p on WS rows.
▬	p on RS rows; k on WS rows.

sl first 3 sts to cn and hold at back; k3; k3 from cn.

First Size Only

Dec row (RS): (K2tog, k1) 3 times; (k2tog, k1, k2tog) 6 times; (k2tog, k1) twice; (k2tog, k1, k2tog) 4 times. 40 sts.

Second Size Only

Dec row (RS): K1; k2tog; k1; (k2tog, k1, k2tog) 13 times. 42 sts.

Third Size Only

Dec row (RS): K2tog; k1; (k2tog, k1, k2tog) 14 times. 44 sts.

All Sizes

Place rem 40[42,44] sts on a holder. With RS facing, rejoin yarn to sts of right side of neck, and keeping continuity, work 1 row in patt without shaping. Dec 1 st at neck edge on next and every foll alt row until 65[69,73] sts rem, so ending with RS facing for next row.

First Size Only

Dec row (RS): (K2tog, k1, k2tog) 4 times; (k1, k2tog) twice; (k2tog, k1, k2tog) 6 times; (k1, k2tog) 3 times. 40 sts.

Second Size Only

Dec row (RS): (K2tog, k1, k2tog) 13 times; k1; k2tog; k1. 42 sts.

Third Size Only

Dec row (RS): (K2tog, k1, k2tog) 14 times; k1; k2tog. 44 sts.

All Sizes

Place rem 40[42,44] sts on a holder.

Back Yoke

With WS facing, rejoin yarn to back yoke sts and keeping continuity, work back and forth in rows until there are same number

THIRD SIZE, CHART C

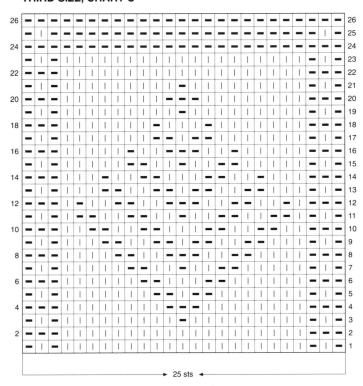

→ 25 sts ←

THIRD SIZE, CHART D

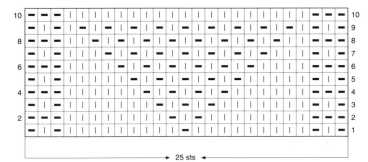

→ 25 sts ←

of rows as front to shoulders, ending with RS facing for next row.

First Size Only

Dec row (RS): (K2tog, k1) 3 times; (k2tog, k1, k2tog) 6 times; (k2tog, k1) twice; (k2tog, k1, k2tog) 4 times; place these last 40 sts on a holder; keeping continuity, work next 66 sts in patt and place these sts on a holder for back neck; (k2tog, k1, k2tog) 4 times; (k1, k2tog) twice; (k2tog, k1, k2tog) 6 times; (k1, k2tog) 3 times; place these last 40 sts on a holder.

Second Size Only

Dec row (RS): K1; k2tog; k1; (k2tog, k1, k2tog) 13 times; place these last 42 sts on a holder; keeping continuity, work next 70 sts in patt and place these sts on a holder for back neck; (k2tog, k1, k2tog) 13 times; k1; k2tog; k1; place these last 42 sts on a holder.

Third Size Only

Dec row (RS): K2tog; k1; (k2tog, k1, k2tog) 14 times; place these last 44 sts on a holder; keeping continuity, work next 74 sts in patt and place these sts on a holder for back neck; (k2tog, k1, k2tog) 14 times; k1; k2tog; place these last 44 sts on a holder.

LEFT SHOULDER STRAP

Place left front and left back shoulder sts on 2 separate double-pointed needles or on 1 circular 3mm (US 3) needle. (**Note:** For circular needle, place sts so that both pointed ends are at neck edge.) With WS facing and a contrasting yarn, using 'thumb method', cast on 20 sts onto neck end of needle holding left back shoulder sts, then turn.

★★Foundation row 1 (RS): With neck end of needle holding left front shoulder sts and using contrasting yarn, k across 20 cast-on sts; turn. Break off contrasting yarn.

Foundation row 2: Join in main yarn and p across first 19 sts of strap; then k last st of strap tog with first st from front shoulder; turn.

Beg with row 1 of chart B, set chart patt on next row as follows—

Chart B row 1 (RS): With yarn at front, sl 1 purlwise; k1; p1; work row 1 of chart B over next 14 sts; p1; k1; p tog (through back loops) last st of strap with first st from back shoulder; turn.

Next row: Sl 1 knitwise; k2; work chart B as set over next 14 sts; k2; k last st of strap tog with next st from front shoulder; turn.

Next row: With yarn at front, sl 1 purlwise; k1; p1; work chart B as set over next 14 sts; p1; k1; p tog (through back loops) last st of strap with next st from back shoulder; turn.

Rep these last 2 rows until all shoulder sts have been incorporated into shoulder strap, so ending after working chart row 1[5,3].

Break off yarn and place 20 strap sts on a holder.★★

RIGHT SHOULDER STRAP

Place right front and right back shoulder sts on needles as for left shoulder strap. With WS facing and a contrasting yarn, using 'thumb method', cast on 20 sts onto neck end of needle holding right front shoulder sts, then turn.

Work as left shoulder strap from ★★ to ★★, but reading 'front shoulder' for 'back shoulder' and vice versa.

NECKBAND

Remove contrasting yarn from shoulder straps and place 20 loops formed by first row of main yarn on 2 holders. With RS facing and 2¾mm (US 2) needles, beg at back st holder and pick up sts as follows—

From back neck holder — k2[0,0]; ★k2tog, k2; rep from ★ to last 4[2,2] sts on holder; k2tog; k2[0,0]; from left shoulder strap — k7; k2tog; k2; k2tog; k7; pick up and k 15[17,19] sts evenly down left side of front neck to front neck holder; from front neck holder — k2[3,1]; ★k2tog, k4; rep from ★ to last 4[5,3] sts on holder; k2tog; k2[3,1]; pick up and k 15[17,19] sts evenly up right side of front neck to right strap holder; from right shoulder strap holder — k7; k2tog; k2; k2tog; k7 to

complete rnd. 156[164,172] sts. Place a st marker on RH needle to mark beg of rnd and working in rnds, work k2, p2 rib for 11.5cm (4½in). Cast off in rib.

SLEEVES

With RS facing and 3mm (US 3) needles, k 19[21,23] sts from gusset holder; pick up and k 72[74,76] sts evenly up armhole edge to shoulder strap; keeping continuity, work across 20 sts of strap in patt; pick up and k 72[74,76] sts evenly down armhole edge to complete rnd. 183[189,195] sts.

Shape Gusset

Place a st marker on RH needle to mark beg of rnd and working in rnds, beg shaping gusset and set sleeve patt as follows—

Next rnd: Ssk; k15[17,19]; k2tog; reading chart A upside down, work last 5[3,1] sts of chart; beg with rnd 2[6,4] and work chart B over next 14 sts; reading chart C upside down, work chart C over next 21[23,25] sts; ★beg with rnd 2[6,4] and work chart B over next 14 sts; reading chart D upside down, work chart D over next 21[23,25] sts★; rep from ★ to ★ once; beg with rnd 2[6,4] and work chart B over next 14 sts; reading chart C upside down, work chart C over next 21[23,25] sts; beg with rnd 2[6,4] and work chart B over next 14 sts; reading chart A upside down, work first 5[3,1] sts of chart.

Cont in patt as set over sleeve sts and working gusset sts in st st throughout, dec 1 st at each side of gusset on every foll 4th rnd until 3 gusset sts in st st rem. 167[171,175] sts.

Work 3 rnds in patt as set without shaping.

Next rnd: Sl 1-k2tog-psso; work in patt to end of rnd.

Next rnd: P1 (seam st); work in patt to end of rnd.

Cont to p seam st, work 2 rnds in patt as set without shaping.

Shape Lower Sleeve

Next rnd: P1 (seam st); k2tog; keeping continuity, work in patt to last 2 sts; ssk. Cont to p seam st to cuff and keeping

*T*he textured vertical panels of the design Stornoway *contain herringbones, trees and a centre panel known as 'heapy' in the North of Scotland. These are interspersed with simple rope cables to produce a lively and interesting design. The style is very traditional, worked in the round with underarm gussets and cabled shoulder straps which extend into the sleeve pattern. Stornoway is knitted in traditional 5-ply gansey wool and is the perfect choice for those looking for a handsome gansey with all the authentic features. Although detailed instructions for working Stornoway are given here, if you are a newcomer to circular knitting, underarm gussets and shoulder straps, it is important that you read the techniques chapter (page 117) before beginning to knit the design.*

continuity of patt as far as possible, dec 1 st at each side of seam st on every foll 3rd rnd until 95[97,97] sts rem.

Work in sleeve patt as set without shaping until sleeve measures 40[42,44]cm (15¾[16½,17¼]in).

Cuff

Dec rnd: (K2tog, k2) 1[5,5] times; (k2tog, k1) 29[19,19] times; (k2tog, k2) 1[5,5] times. 64[68,68] sts.

Change to 2¾mm (US 2) and work k2, p2 rib for 6[6,7]cm (2½[2½,2¾]in).

Cast off in rib.

FINISHING

Darn in loose ends. Rinse, short spin and dry garment on a woolly board (see page 124). Do not press.

A = 113[121,128]cm   45[48,51]in

B = 65[67.5,70]cm   25½[26½,27½]in

C = 31[32.5,33]cm   12¼[12¾,13]in

D = 25[25.5,26]cm   9¾[10,10¼]in

E = 46[48,51]cm   18¼[19,20]in

ERISKAY

SIZES

To fit small [medium, large]
Directions for larger sizes are given in brackets. Where there is only one set of figures, it applies to all sizes.

KNITTED MEASUREMENTS

Underarm, excluding gussets
103[113.5,124]cm (41¼[45½,49½]in)
Length 62[65,67]cm (24¾[25¾,26¾]in)
Sleeve length 46[47,48]cm (18[18½,19]in)

MATERIALS

Yarn weight used: 5-ply gansey wool (US sport)
9[10,11] x 100g (3½oz) balls of Alice Starmore's *Scottish Fleet* in Red
1 set of double-pointed *or* circular 2¼mm (US 1) and 2¾mm (US 2) needles
1 cable needle
8 stitch holders
Stitch markers

TENSION (GAUGE)

31 sts and 43 rows to 10cm (4in) measured over st st, using 2¾mm (US 2) needles (see note below)

SPECIAL NOTE

The sweater is entirely patterned throughout. The st st tension (gauge) swatch simply makes it easier to accurately measure the tension (gauge).

BODY

Body is worked in one piece to armhole.
With 2¼mm (US 1) needles, cast on 290[320,346] sts.
Place a st marker on RH needle to mark beg of rnd, then making sure cast-on edge is not twisted and working in rnds (RS always facing), work k1, p1 rib for 6cm (2½in), slipping marker on each rnd.

First Size Only
Inc rnd: *(M1, k10) twice; m1; k9; rep from * to end of rnd. 320 sts.

Second Size Only
Inc rnd: *M1; k10; rep from * to end of rnd. 352 sts.

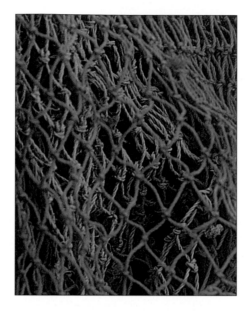

*T*he island of Eriskay, in the outer Hebrides, is the home of the most ornately patterned gansey in the British Isles. The traditional idea served as the basis for Eriskay. It proved to be a mathematical tour de force and was a joy to design.

Third Size Only
Inc rnd: M1; k10; (m1, k9) 17 times; (m1, k10) twice; (m1, k9) 17 times; m1; k10. 384 sts.

All Sizes
Change to 2¾mm (US 2) needles and reading chart from right to left, set chart A patt as follows—
Chart A rnd 1: Rep 16 patt sts of rnd 1 of chart A 20[22,24] times.
Reading every chart rnd from right to left, cont in chart A patt as set, rep 10 patt rnds, until 105[111,117] rnds in total of chart A have been completed, slipping marker on every rnd throughout.

Begin Gussets
Next rnd: Keeping marker in place to mark first st for beg of rnd and beg of first

underarm gusset, *m1; k1; m1; keeping continuity, work 159[175,191] sts in patt*; place a st marker on RH needle to mark next st for beg of 2nd underarm gusset, then rep from * to * once more. (The k st and the inc sts form the gussets – there are now 3 sts in each gusset.)
Working all gusset sts in st st throughout, inc 1 st at each side of each gusset on every foll 4th rnd until there are 9[11,13] sts in each gusset, AND AT THE SAME TIME cont to work chart A patt as set over the 159[175,191] sts of front and over the 159[175,191] sts of back until 120[130,140] rnds in total of chart A have been completed.
Set chart B patt as follows—
Chart B rnd 1: *K9[11,13] gusset sts; p1; work rnd 1 of chart B over next 157[173,189] sts, working first 0[2,1] sts of chart as indicated, rep 6 patt sts 26[28,31] times, and working last 1[3,2] sts of chart as indicated; p1; rep from * once more.
Cont in chart B patt as set over front and back sts, inc 1 st at each side of gusset on next and every foll 4th rnd until there are 19[21,23] sts in each gusset and all 18 rnds of chart B have been completed. 356[392,428] sts.

Divide for Yokes
Place first 19[21,23] sts of rnd (gusset) on a holder, leave next 159[175,191] sts (front yoke sts) on a spare needle, place next 19[21,23] sts (gusset) on a holder. 159[175,191] sts of back yoke rem.

Back Yoke
Beg with a WS row and working back and forth in rows, inc across 159[175,191] sts of back yoke as follows—
★First Size Only
Inc row (WS): P2; k29; *p2; k11; p2; k1; m1; k2; m1; k1; p2; k11; p2; k29; rep from * once more; p2. 163 sts.

Second Size Only
Inc row (WS): P2; k29; *p2; k11; (p2; k3; m1; k2) twice; p2; k11; p2; k29; rep from * once more; p2. 179 sts.

Third Size Only
Inc row (WS): P2; k29; *p2; k5; k2tog; k5; (p2; k3; m1; k2) 3 times; p2; k11; p2; k29; rep from * once more; p2. 195 sts.

CHART A

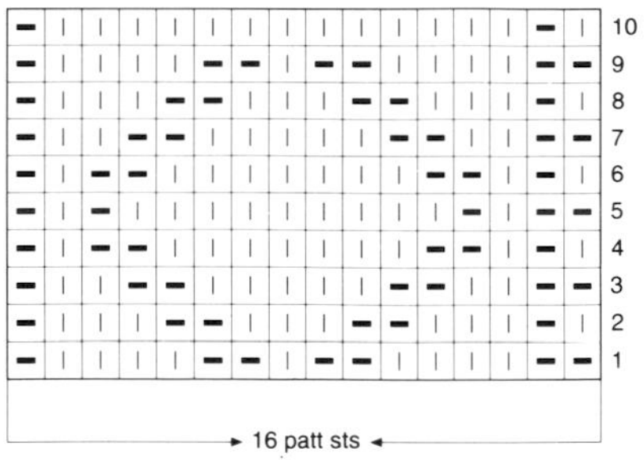

→ 16 patt sts ←

CHART B

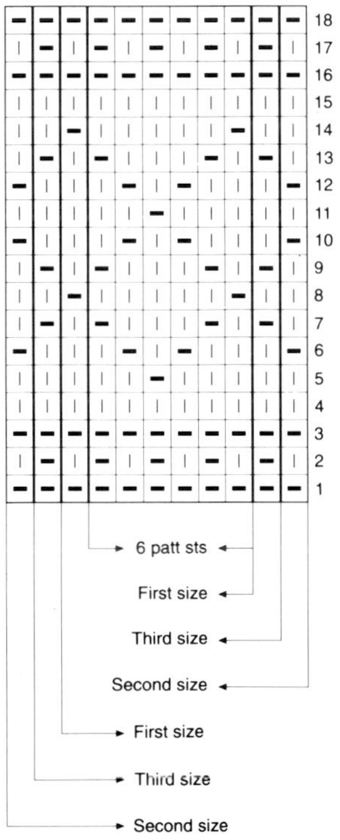

→ 6 patt sts ←

First size ←

Third size ←

Second size ←

→ First size

→ Third size

→ Second size

CHART C

→ 33 sts ←

KEY

| | k on RS rows; p on WS rows.

− p on RS rows; k on WS rows.

sl first 3 sts to cn and hold at back; k3; k3 from cn.

sl first 3 sts to cn and hold at front; k3; k3 from cn.

○ yo.

╱ k2tog.

ᐠ ssk.

⋀ sl 1 – k2tog – psso.

CHART D

→ 11 sts ←

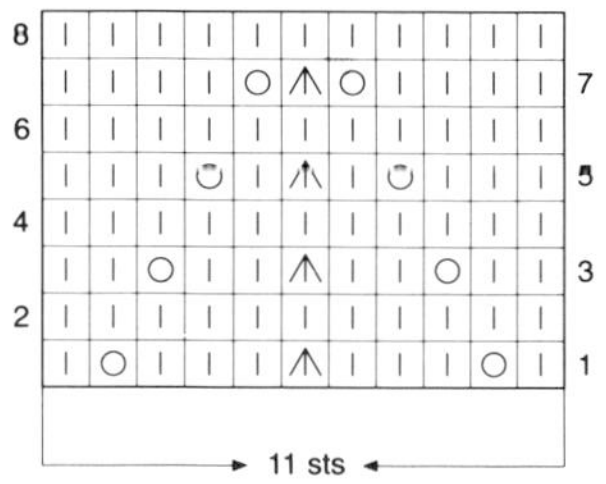

CHART K

→ 13 sts ←

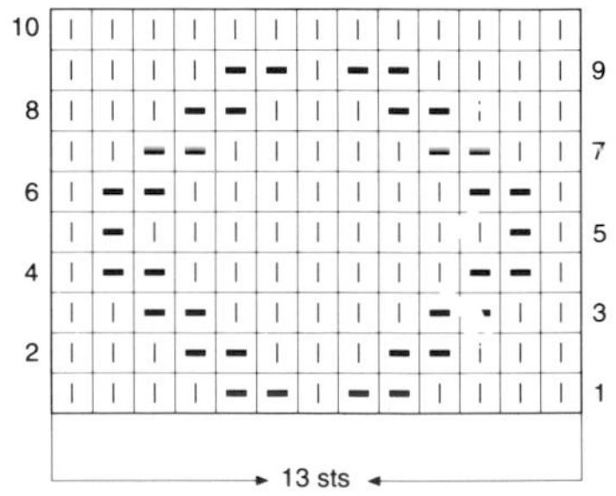

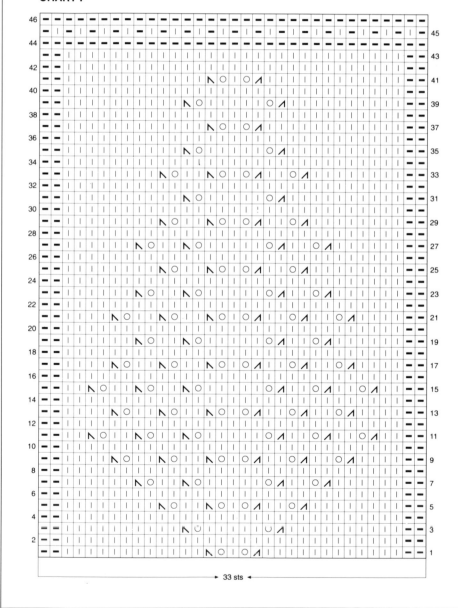

CHART E

First size, 10 sts

Second size, 18 sts

Third size, 26 sts

CHART F

33 sts

All Sizes

Reading charts from right to left for RS (odd-numbered) rows and from left to right for WS (even-numbered) rows and beg all charts from row 1, set yoke patt as follows—

Chart row 1 (RS): Work chart C over first 33 sts; work chart D over next 11 sts; work chart E over next 10[18,26] sts; work chart D over next 11 sts; work chart F over next 33 sts; work chart D over next 11 sts; work chart G over next 10[18,26] sts; work chart D over next 11 sts; work chart C over last 33 sts.

Cont in patts as set and rep all rows of charts D, E and G, work until all 46 rows of charts C and F have been completed.★★

Cont working charts D, E and G as set and work chart H over first and last 33 sts and chart I over centre 33 sts until all 43 rows of charts H and I have been completed, so ending with WS facing for next row.

K 1 row (WS).

Next row: ★K1, p1; rep from ★ to last st; k1.

K 1 row.

Dec row (RS): ★K2; (k2tog, k1) 18[20,22] times; k2; place these last 40[44,48] sts on a holder★; k next 47[51,55] sts and place these sts on a holder for back neck; k2; (k1, k2tog) 18[20,22] times; k2; place these last 40[44,48] sts on a holder.

Front Yoke

With WS facing, rejoin yarn to 159[175, 191] sts of front yoke and working back and forth in rows, work as back from ★★ to ★★.

Cont working charts D, E and G as set and work chart H over first and last 33 sts and chart J over centre 33 sts until all 36 rows of chart J have been completed, so ending with RS facing for next row.

Shape Front Neck

Next row (RS): Keeping continuity, work 67[74,81] sts in patt; place next 29[31,33] sts on a holder for front neck; turn, leaving rem sts on a spare needle. Keeping continuity of patt throughout, shape left side of neck as follows—

★★★Cast off 3 sts at beg of next row.

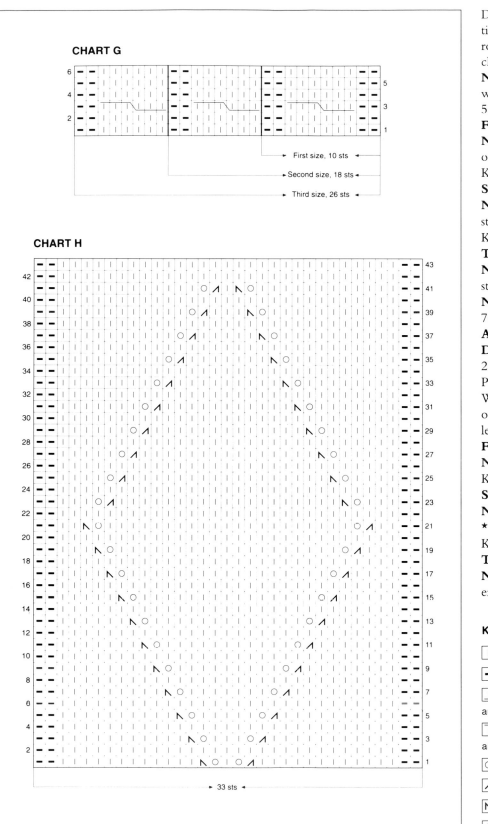

CHART G

First size, 10 sts

Second size, 18 sts

Third size, 26 sts

CHART H

33 sts

Dec 1 st at neck edge on every foll row 5 times, ending with WS facing for next row. 59[66,73] sts rem and 43 rows of chart H have been completed.

Next row (WS): K to end of row, working k2tog at neck edge. 58[65,72] sts.★★★

First Size Only

Next row: *K1, p1; rep from * to end of row.

K 1 row.

Second Size Only

Next row: *K1, p1; rep from * to last 3 sts; k1; p2tog. 64 sts.

K 1 row.

Third Size Only

Next row: *K1, p1; rep from * to last 2 sts; k2tog.

Next row: K2tog; k to end of row. 70 sts.

All Sizes

Dec row (RS): K2; (k2tog, k1) 18[20, 22] times; k2.

Place rem 40[44,48] sts on a holder.

With RS facing, rejoin yarn to right side of neck and keeping continuity, shape as left side of neck from ★★★ to ★★★.

First Size Only

Next row: *P1, k1; rep from * to end.

K 1 row.

Second Size Only

Next row: P2tog; k1; *p1, k1; rep from * to end of row. 64 sts.

K 1 row.

Third Size Only

Next row: K2tog; *p1, k1; rep from * to end of row.

KEY

| | k on RS rows; p on WS rows.

| − | p on RS rows; k on WS rows.

sl first 3 sts to cn and hold at back; k3; k3 from cn.

sl first 3 sts to cn and hold at front; k3; k3 from cn.

| O | yo.

| ⟋ | k2tog.

| ⟍ | ssk.

| ⋀ | sl 1 – k2tog – psso.

Next row: K to last 2 sts; k2tog. 70 sts.
All Sizes
Dec row (RS): K2; (k1, k2tog) 18[20, 22] times; k2.
Place rem 40[44,48] sts on a holder.

LEFT SHOULDER STRAP

Place left front and left back shoulder sts on 2 separate double-pointed needles or on 1 circular 2¾mm (US 2) needle. (**Note:** For circular needle, place sts so that both pointed ends are at neck edge.) With WS facing and a contrasting yarn,

*W*orked in, traditional 5-ply gansey wool, Eriskay *is a truly magnificent gansey and an ideal project for the knitter who craves an interesting challenge. The reward is a garment of heirloom quality. (See page 127 for yarn information and suppliers' addresses.)*

*T*he main body, shoulder straps and sleeves of Eriskay *are worked in a vertical starfish pattern. The yoke (pictured left) is bordered with a small diamond pattern, and for the yoke I have designed blocks containing trees, anchors, diamonds and stars. An openwork horse-shoe pattern and rope cables are set between the block panels. The small size, modelled here, has single cables worked in the yoke, whilst the second and third sizes have two and three cables respectively.*

using 'thumb method', cast on 15 sts onto neck end of needle holding left back shoulder sts, then turn.

★★Foundation row 1 (RS): With neck end of needle holding left front shoulder sts and using contrasting yarn, k across 15 cast-on sts; turn.

Break off contrasting yarn.

Foundation row 2: Join in main yarn and p across first 14 sts of strap; then ssk last st of strap tog with first st from front shoulder; turn.

Beg with row 1 of chart K, set chart patt on next row as follows—

Chart K row 1 (RS): With yarn at front, sl 1 purlwise; work row 1 of chart K over next 13 sts; p last st of strap tog with first st from back shoulder; turn.

Next row: Sl 1 knitwise; work chart K as set over next 13 sts; ssk last st of strap tog with next st from front shoulder; turn.

Next row: With yarn at front, sl 1 purlwise; work chart K as set over next 13 sts; p last st of strap tog with next st from back shoulder; turn.

Rep these last 2 rows until all shoulder sts have been incorporated into shoulder strap, so ending on chart row 9[7,5] inclusive.

Break off yarn and place 15 strap sts on a holder.★★

RIGHT SHOULDER STRAP

Place right front and right back shoulder sts on needles as for left shoulder strap. With WS facing and a contrasting yarn, using 'thumb method', cast on 15 sts onto neck end of needle holding right front shoulder sts, then turn.

Work as left shoulder strap from ★★ to ★★, but reading 'front shoulder' for 'back shoulder' and vice versa.

NECKBAND

Remove contrasting yarn from shoulder straps and place 15 loops formed by first row of main yarn on 2 holders.

With RS facing and 2¼mm (US 1) needles, beg at back neck and k 47[51,55] sts from back neck holder; k 15 sts from left shoulder strap holder; pick up and k

10 sts evenly down left side of front neck; k 29[31,33] sts from front neck holder; pick up and k 10 sts evenly up right side of front neck; k 15 sts from right shoulder strap holder to complete rnd. 126[132,138] sts.

Place a st marker on RH needle to mark beg of rnd and working in rnds, work k1, p1 rib for 3[4,4]cm (1½[1¾,1¾]in). Cast off in rib.

SLEEVES

With RS facing and 2¼mm (US 2)

needles, k 19[21,23] sts from gusset holder; pick up and k 73 sts evenly up armhole edge to shoulder strap; work sts from shoulder strap as follows—

Keeping continuity, p1; work rnd 10[8,6] of chart K across next 13 sts; p1; pick up and k 73 sts evenly down armhole edge to complete rnd. 180[182,184] sts.

Shape Gusset

Place a st marker on RH needle to mark beg of rnd and working in rnds, beg shaping gusset and set patt as follows—

Next rnd: Ssk; k15[17,19]; k2tog; p1;

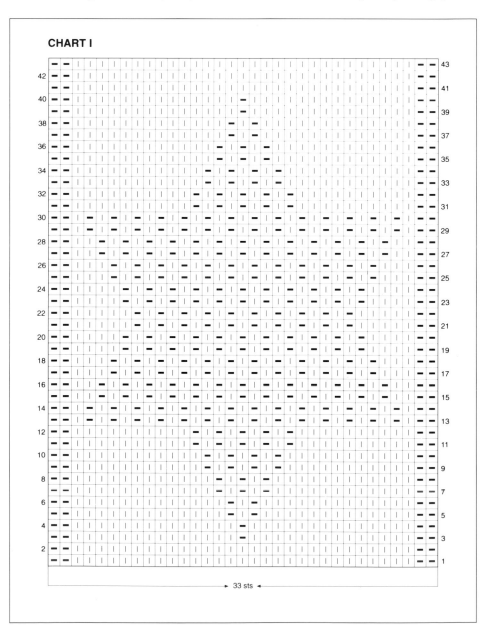

CHART I

33 sts

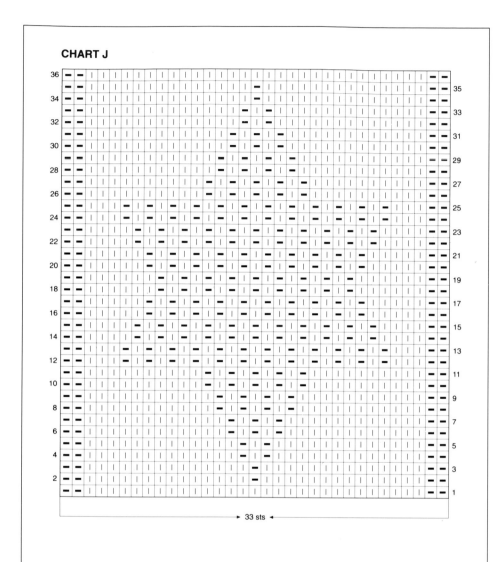

CHART J

33 sts

work last 7 sts of rnd 1[9,7] of chart A; rep 16 patt sts of same rnd 9 times; work first 8 sts of patt rep; p1.

Cont in chart A patt as set and working gusset sts in st st throughout, dec 1 st at each side of gusset on every foll 4th rnd until 3 gusset sts in st st rem. 164 sts.

Work 3 rnds in patt A without shaping.

Next rnd: Sl 1–k2tog–psso; work in patt to end of rnd.

Next rnd: P1 (seam st); work in patt to end of rnd.

Cont to p seam st, work 2 rnds in patt as set without shaping.

Shape Lower Sleeve

Next rnd: P1 (seam st); k2tog; keeping continuity, work in patt to last 2 sts; ssk.

Cont to p seam st to cuff and keeping continuity of patt, dec 1 st at each side of seam st on every foll 4th rnd until 130[126,122] sts rem, then on every foll 3rd rnd until 82[84,86] sts rem.

Work as set without shaping until sleeve measures 40[41,42]cm (15½[16,16½]in).

Cuff

Dec rnd: K1[2,3]; *k2tog, k2; rep from * to last 1[2,3] sts; k1[2,3]. 62[64,66] sts.

Change to 2¼mm (US 1) needles and work k1, p1 rib for 6cm (2½in). Cast off.

FINISHING

Darn in loose ends. Rinse, short spin and dry garment on a woolly board (see page 124). Do not press.

KEY

	k on RS rows; p on WS rows.
–	p on RS rows; k on WS rows.

sl first 3 sts to cn and hold at back; k3; k3 from cn.

sl first 3 sts to cn and hold at front; k3; k3 from cn.

○	yo.
⟋	k2tog.
⟍	ssk.
⟋⟍	sl 1 – k2tog – psso.

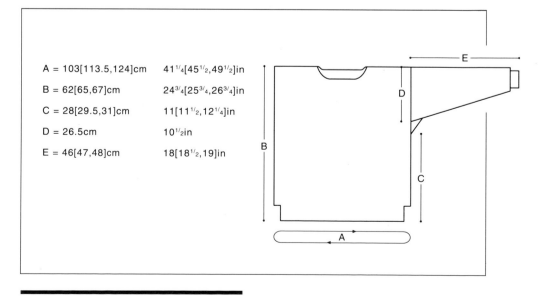

A = 103[113.5,124]cm   41¼[45½,49½]in

B = 62[65,67]cm   24¾[25¾,26¾]in

C = 28[29.5,31]cm   11[11½,12¼]in

D = 26.5cm   10½in

E = 46[47,48]cm   18[18½,19]in

LOCHINVER

RATING ★ ★

SIZES
To fit small [medium, large]
Directions for larger sizes are given in brackets. Where there is only one set of figures, it applies to all sizes.

KNITTED MEASUREMENTS
Underarm, excluding gussets
106[112,118.5]cm (42½[45,47½]in)
Length 67[68,69]cm (26½[27,27½]in)
Sleeve length 46[47,48]cm (18[18½,19]in)

MATERIALS
Yarn weight used: double knitting wool (US knitting worsted)
14[15,16] x 50g (1¾oz) balls of Rowan *Designer DK* in shade no. 672 Kingfisher Blue
1 set of double-pointed *or* circular 3¾mm (US 5) needles
1 set of double-pointed 3¼mm (US 3) needles
6 stitch holders
Stitch markers
3 buttons

TENSION (GAUGE)
26 sts and 34 rows to 10cm (4in) measured over chart F patt, using 3¾mm (US 5) needles

BODY
Back and front lower border flaps are worked separately first, then they are joined and body is worked in one piece to armhole.
Border Flaps
With 3¾mm (US 5) needles, cast on 138[146,154] sts.
Working back and forth in rows, work first 8 rows of lower border as follows—
P 1 row (RS); k 2 rows; p 2 rows; k 2 rows; p 1 row.
Reading chart from right to left for RS (odd-numbered) rows and from left to right for WS (even-numbered) rows, set chart A patt as follows—
Chart A row 1 (RS): Work 8 sts of row 1 of chart A as indicated; rep 4 patt sts

*M*any of the original Scottish ganseys featured horizontal patterned bands that were worked on yokes and sleeve tops. I have played with this format in Lochinver by placing horizontal bands on the main body and interspersing them with stocking stitch on the sleeves. The yoke is worked in a small wave pattern, which contrasts well with the shoulder strap panels.

30[32,34] times; work last 10 sts of chart as indicated.
Chart A row 2: Work first 10 sts of row 2 of chart A as indicated; rep 4 patt sts 30[32,34] times; work last 8 sts of chart as indicated.
Cont in chart A patt as set, rep 4 patt rows 5 times in all, then work chart rows 1 and 2 once more, thus working 22 chart A rows in total.
K 2 rows; p 2 rows, so ending with RS facing for next row.
Break off yarn and leave border flap sts on a spare needle.

Work a second identical border flap, but do not break off yarn.
Join Border Flaps
With RS facing, p first st of second border flap; k across rem sts of this flap; with RS of first border facing, p first st; k across rem sts of this flap. 276[292,308] sts.
With RS still facing, join borders into a circle and work first rnd as follows—
Rnd 1: Place a st marker on RH needle to mark first st as beg of rnd and underarm seam st, *p1 (seam st); p137[145,153]*; place a st marker on RH needle to mark next st for centre of rnd and underarm seam st, rep from * to * once more.
Working in rnds (RS always facing) and keeping markers in place on every rnd throughout, p 1 rnd more.
Next rnd: *P seam st; k137[145,153]; rep from * once more.
Reading all chart rnds from right to left, set chart B patt as follows—
Chart B rnd 1: *P seam st; rep 4 patt sts of rnd 1 of chart B 34[36,38] times; work last st of chart as indicated; rep from * once more.
Cont to p seam sts and cont in chart B patt as set, rep 6 patt rnds 3 times in all, then work chart rnds 1 through 4 once more, thus working 22 chart B rnds in total.
Cont to p seam sts throughout, k 1 rnd; p 2 rnds; k 2 rnds; p 2 rnds; k 1 rnd.
Set chart C patt as follows—
Chart C rnd 1 (RS): *P seam st; rep 8 patt sts of rnd 1 of chart C 17[18,19] times; work last st of chart as indicated; rep from * once more.
Cont in chart C patt as set, rep 4 patt rnds 5 times in all, then work chart rnds 1 and 2 once more, thus working 22 chart C rnds in total.
Work 8 rnds as between chart B and C patts from ** to **.
Set chart D patt as follows—
Chart D rnd 1: *P seam st; rep 2 patt sts of rnd 1 of chart D 68[72,76] times; work last st of chart as indicated; rep from * once more.
Cont in chart D patt as set, rep 2 patt rnds 11 times in all, thus working 22 chart C rnds in total.

CHART A

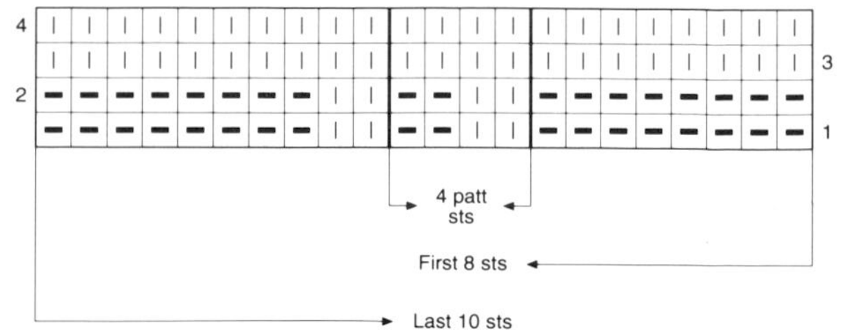

4
2
3
1

4 patt sts

First 8 sts

Last 10 sts

CHART B

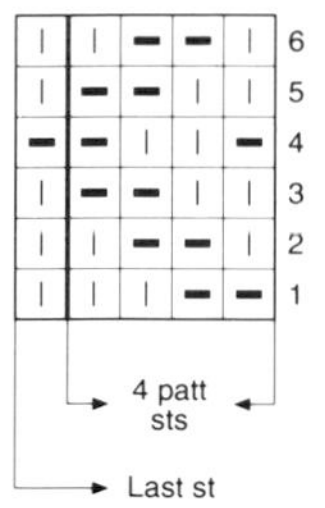

6
5
4
3
2
1

4 patt sts

Last st

CHART C

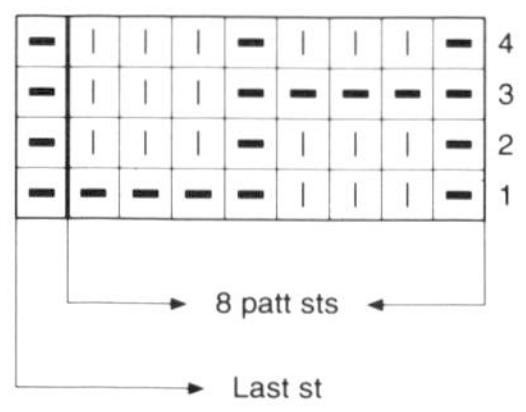

4
3
2
1

8 patt sts

Last st

CHART D

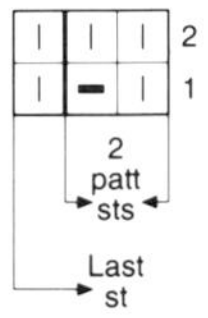

2
1

2 patt sts

Last st

CHART E

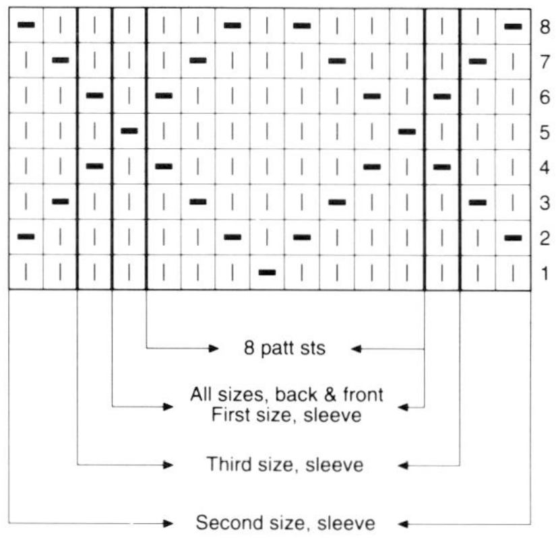

8
7
6
5
4
3
2
1

8 patt sts

All sizes, back & front
First size, sleeve

Third size, sleeve

Second size, sleeve

CHART F

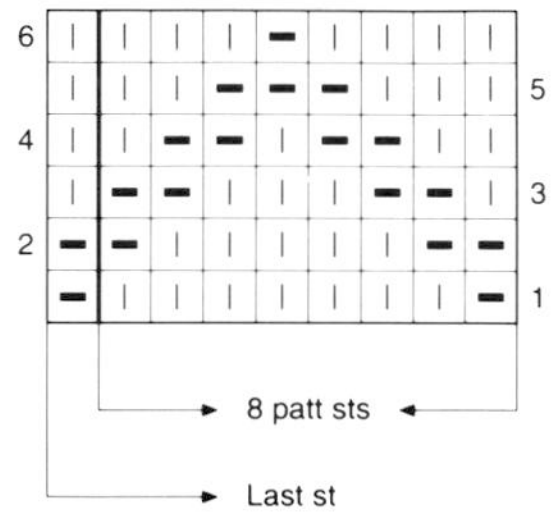

6
4
2
5
3
1

8 patt sts

Last st

CHART G

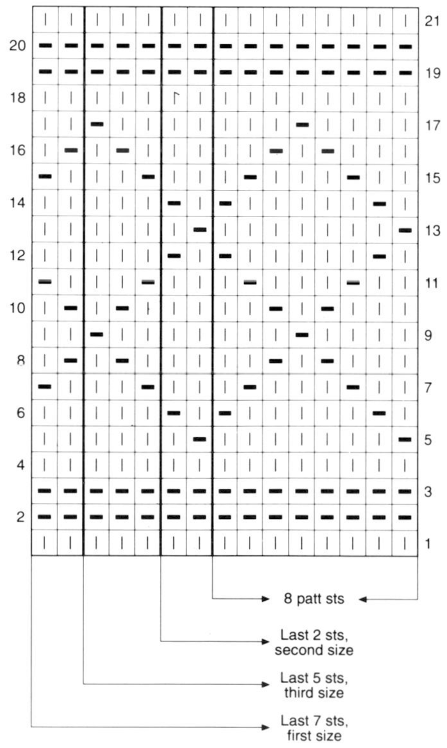

21
20
19
18
17
16
15
14
13
12
11
10
9
8
7
6
5
4
3
2
1

8 patt sts

Last 2 sts,
second size

Last 5 sts,
third size

Last 7 sts,
first size

KEY

| | k on RS rows; p on WS rows.

— p on RS rows; k on WS rows.

CHART H

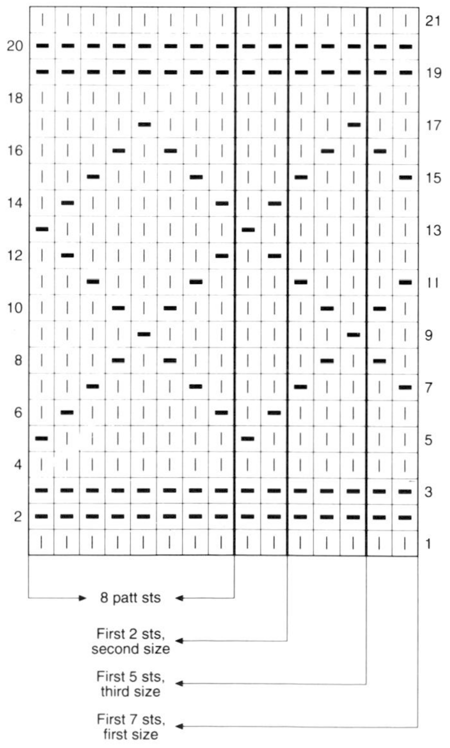

21
20
19
18
17
16
15
14
13
12
11
10
9
8
7
6
5
4
3
2
1

8 patt sts

First 2 sts,
second size

First 5 sts,
third size

First 7 sts,
first size

Work 8 rnds as between chart B and C patts from ★★ to ★★.

Begin Gussets

Beg gussets and set chart E patt as follows—

Chart E rnd 1: ★M1; k seam st; m1; rep 8 patt sts of rnd 1 of chart E 17[18,19] times; work last st of chart as indicated; rep from ★ once more. (The seam st and inc sts form the gussets – there are now 3 sts in each gusset.)

Working all gusset sts in st st throughout, inc 1 st at each side of each gusset on every foll 3rd rnd until there are 21 sts in each gusset, AND AT THE SAME TIME work patt over back and front sts as follows—

Cont in chart E patt as set, rep 8 patt rnds 3 times in all, work chart rnd 1 once more, thus working 25 chart E rnds in total, then k 1 rnd, p 2 rnds (keeping gusset sts in st st). 316[332,348] sts.

Divide for Yokes

Place first 21 sts of rnd (gusset) on a holder, leave next 137[145,153] sts (back yoke sts) on a spare needle, place next 21 sts (gusset) on a holder. 137[145,153] sts of front yoke rem.

Front Yoke

Beg with a WS row and working back and forth in rows, p 1 row, k 2 rows, p 2 rows, so ending with RS facing for next row.

Reading chart from right to left chart for RS (odd-numbered) rows and from left to right for WS (even-numbered) rows, set chart F patt as follows—

Chart F row 1 (RS): Rep 8 patt sts of row 1 of chart F 17[18,19] times; work last st of chart as indicated.

Chart F row 2: Work first st of row 2 of chart F as indicated; rep 8 patt sts 17[18,19] times.

Cont in chart F patt as set, rep 6 patt rows until yoke measures 15.5[16.5,17.5]cm (6¼[6½,7]in) from top of gussets, ending with RS facing for next row.

Shape Front Neck

Next row (RS): Keeping continuity of patt, work 62[65,68] sts in patt; place next 13[15,17] sts on a holder for front neck; turn, leaving rem sts on a spare needle.

*T*he neatly buttoned neckband of Lochinver *echoes those of past ganseys, though here the finished look is contemporary and decidedly feminine. The man pictured above is wearing* Stornoway. *(Instructions for the* Stornoway *design are given on page 11).*

Keeping continuity of chart F patt, shape left side of neck as follows—

★★★Cast off 3 sts at beg of next row.
Work 1 row without shaping.
Cast off 2 sts at beg of next and foll alt row. 55[58,61] sts rem.
Dec 1 st at neck edge on every foll row 6 times.
Work 1 row without shaping.★★★
Dec 1 st at neck edge on next and foll alt row, so ending with RS facing for next row. 47[50,53] sts rem.

Left Shoulder Strap

Set chart G patt as follows—

Chart G row 1 (RS): Rep 8 patt sts of row 1 of chart G 5[6,6] times; work last 7[2,5] sts of chart as indicated.

Chart G row 2: Work first 7[2,5] sts of row 2 of chart G as indicated; rep 8 patt sts 5[6,6] times.

Cont in chart G patt as set until all 21 chart rows have been completed.
Place sts on a holder.

With RS facing, rejoin yarn to 62[65,68] sts of right side of neck and keeping continuity of chart F patt to shoulder strap, work 2 rows without shaping, then shape as left side of front neck from ★★★ to ★★★.

Dec 1 st at neck edge on next row. 48[51,54] sts rem.

Work 1 row without shaping, so ending with RS facing for next row.

Right Shoulder Strap

Work shoulder strap as left side of front neck, but foll chart H (instead of chart G), beg and ending rows as indicated on chart

H and dec 1 st at beg of first chart row. Place rem 47[50,53] sts on a holder.

Back Yoke

With WS facing, rejoin yarn to 137[145, 153] sts of back yoke and beg with a WS row and working back and forth in rows, p 1 row, k 2 rows, p 2 rows, so ending with RS facing for next row.

Work in chart F patt as front yoke, rep 6 patt rows until there are same number of chart F patt rows as front yoke to beg of shoulder strap, ending with RS facing for next row.

Place first 47[50,53] sts on a spare needle, leave centre 43[45,47] sts on a holder for back neck, place rem 47[50,53] sts on a spare needle.

SLEEVES

Before beg sleeves, graft back shoulder sts to front shoulder strap sts. (See page 121 for grafting.)

Begin Sleeve

With RS facing and 3¼mm (US 5) needles, k 21 sts from gusset holder; pick up and k 121[127,131] sts evenly around armhole edge to complete rnd. 142[148,152] sts.

Shape Gusset

Place a st marker on RH needle to mark beg of rnd and working in rnds, beg shaping gusset as follows—

Next rnd: Ssk; k next 17 gusset sts; k2tog; p121[127,131].

Next rnd: K 19 gusset sts; p121[127,131]. K 1 rnd without shaping.

Cont shaping gussets and set chart E patt as follows—

Chart E rnd 1: Ssk; k15; k2tog; work first 0[3,1] sts of rnd 1 of chart E as indicated; rep 8 patt sts 15[15,16] times; work last 1[4,2] sts of chart as indicated.

Cont in chart E patt as set over sleeve sts, rep 8 patt rnds twice in all, work chart rnds 1 through 6 once more, thus working 22 chart E rnds in total, AND AT THE SAME TIME working gusset sts in st st throughout, shape gussets by dec 1 st at each side of gusset on every foll 3rd rnd until 3 gusset sts in st st rem. 124[130,134] sts.

Work 2 rnds in chart E patt as set without shaping.

Next rnd: Sl 1-k2tog-psso; work in chart E patt to end of rnd.

Next rnd: P1 (seam st); k to end of rnd. P 1 rnd.

Shape Lower Sleeve

Next rnd: P1 (seam st); k2tog; p to last 2 sts; ssk.

Cont to p seam st to cuff, k 2 rnds.

Dec 1 st at each side of seam st on next and every foll 3rd row AND AT THE SAME TIME cont to p seam st and work sleeve sts in patt as follows—

K 12[14,14] rnds; p 2 rnds; k 1 rnd.

Work chart C, rep 4 patt rnds 5 times in all, then work rnds 1 and 2 once more,

thus working 22 chart C rnds in total. K 1 rnd; p 2 rnds; k 14[16,16] rnds; p 2 rnds; k 1 rnd.

Work chart B, rep 6 patt rnds 3 times in all, then work rnds 1 through 4 once more, thus working 22 chart B rnds in total.

K 1 rnd; p 2 rnds.

Work in st st only over sleeve sts and cont to dec on every 3rd rnd as set until 60[64,66] sts rem.

Work in st st without shaping until sleeve measures 39[40,41]cm (15¼[15¾,16¼]in).

Cuff

Dec rnd: K0[0,1]; (k2tog, k8[6,6]) 6[8,8] times; k0[0,1]. 54[56,58] sts.

Change to 3¼mm (US 3) needles and work k1, p1 rib for 7cm (2¾in).

Cast off in rib.

NECKBAND

With RS facing and 3¼mm (US 3) needles, beg at centre of left shoulder strap and pick up and k 24 sts evenly down left side of front neck to front neck holder; k 13[15,17] sts from front neck holder; pick up and k 32 sts up right front neck to back neck holder; k 43[45,47] sts from back neck holder; pick up and k 8 sts to centre of left shoulder strap; then cast on 7 sts onto RH needle. 127[131,135] sts.

Work back and forth in rows as follows—

Row 1 (WS): P6; *k1, p1; rep from * to last 7 sts; p7.

Row 2: P1; *k1, p1; rep from * to end of row.

Rep these 2 rows until 16 rows in total have been completed, AND AT THE SAME TIME make buttonholes on 4th, 12th and 20th rows as follows—

Butthonhole row (RS): P1; k1; p1; yo; k2tog; *k1, p1; rep from * to end of row. Keeping continuity of rib patt, work 3 rows without shaping.

Cast off in rib.

FINISHING

Sew cast on edge of 7 extra sts on neckband to inside of neckline. Sew on buttons. Rinse, short spin and dry garment on a woolly board (see page 124). Do not press.

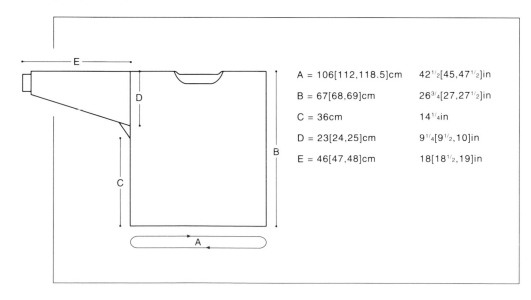

A = 106[112,118.5]cm	42½[45,47½]in
B = 67[68,69]cm	26¾[27,27½]in
C = 36cm	14¼in
D = 23[24,25]cm	9¼[9½,10]in
E = 46[47,48]cm	18[18½,19]in

FIFE

SIZE

One size only to fit age 8-10 years or 68-72cm (27-28½in) chest

KNITTED MEASUREMENTS

Underarm, excluding gussets 91cm (36in)
Length 48cm (19in)
Sleeve length 36cm (14¼in)

MATERIALS

Yarn weight used: 5-ply gansey wool (US sport)
6 x 100g (3½oz) balls of Alice Starmore's *Scottish Fleet* in Natural
1 set of double-pointed *or* circular 2¾mm (US 2) and 3mm (US 3) needles
8 stitch holders
Stitch markers

TENSION (GAUGE)

15 sts and 20 rows to 5cm (2in) measured over st st, using 3mm (US 3) needles

SPECIAL NOTE

Yarn is used double for cast-on and cast-off edges only.

BODY

Body is worked in one piece to armhole.
With 2¾mm (US 2) needles and yarn doubled, cast on 264 sts.
Place a st marker on RH needle to mark beg of rnd, then making sure cast-on edge is not twisted, using yarn single throughout and working in rnds (RS always facing), work k2, p2 rib for 5cm (2in), slipping marker on each rnd.
Inc rnd: *M1, k11; rep from * to end of rnd. 288 sts.
Change to 3mm (US 3) needles and reading chart from right to left, set patt as follows—
Chart rnd 1: Keeping marker in place to mark first st for beg of rnd and underarm seam st, *work first 4 sts of chart as indicated; rep 42 patt sts 3 times; work last 14 sts of chart as indicated*; place a st marker on RH needle to mark next st for centre of rnd and underarm seam st, then

*T*he fisher gansey designed for a particular individual, as I mentioned in my introduction, is epitomised by Fife. To work this pattern in any other child's size would require altering the pattern panels, and so it comes in only one size.

rep from * to * once more.
Reading every chart rnd from right to left, cont in chart patt as set, rep 40 patt rnds until body measures 24cm (9½in) from beg, slipping markers on every rnd throughout and ending with an odd-numbered chart rnd facing for next rnd.
Begin Gussets
Next rnd: Slip marker, m1; k seam st; m1; keeping continuity, work in patt as set to next underarm seam st; slip marker, m1; k seam st; m1; keeping continuity, work in patt as set to end of rnd. (The seam st and inc sts form the gussets – there are now 3 sts in each gusset.)
Cont to work chart patt as set over 143 sts of back and 143 sts of front, and working all gusset sts in st st, inc 1 st at each side of each gusset on every foll 4th rnd until

there are 17 sts in each gusset, so ending after working an odd-numbered chart rnd. 320 sts.
Divide for Yokes
Place first 17 sts of rnd (gusset) on a holder, leave next 143 sts (back yoke sts) on a spare needle, place next 17 sts (gusset) on a holder. 143 sts of front yoke rem.
Front Yoke
Beg with a WS row and keeping continuity, work 143 sts of front yoke in patt, working back and forth in rows (now reading WS chart rows from left to right and RS rows from right to left) until yoke measures 11.5cm (4½in) from top of gussets, ending with RS facing for next row.
Shape Front Neck
Next row (RS): Keeping continuity, work 60 sts in patt; place next 23 sts on a holder; turn, leaving rem sts on a spare needle.
Keeping continuity of patt throughout, shape left side of neck as follows—
**Cast off 3 sts at beg of next row. 57 sts.
Work 1 row without shaping.
Cast off 2 sts at beg of next row. 55 sts.
Dec 1 st at neck edge on every foll row 5 times, then at same edge on every foll alt row 4 times. 46 sts rem***, so ending with WS facing for next row.
Next row (WS): P1; *p2tog, p1; rep from * to end of row.
Place rem 31 sts on a holder.
With RS facing, rejoin yarn to sts of right side of neck, and keeping continuity, work 2 rows in patt without shaping, then shape as left side of neck from ** to ***, so ending with RS facing for next row.
Next row (RS): K1; *k2tog, k1; rep from * to end of row.
Place rem 31 sts on a holder.
Back Yoke
With WS facing, rejoin yarn to 143 sts of back yoke and keeping continuity, work in patt as set, working back and forth in rows until there are same number of chart rows as right front, so ending with RS facing for next row.
Next row (RS): K1; *k2tog, k1; rep from * 15 times in all and place these

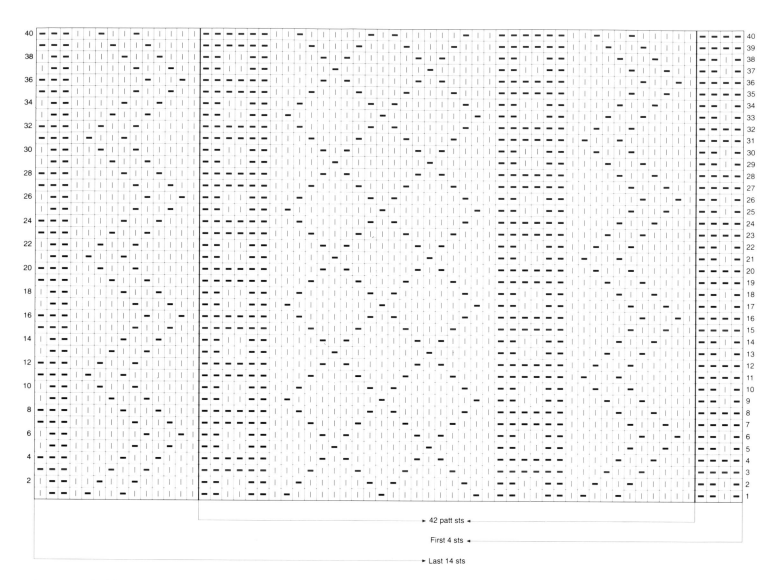

► 42 patt sts ◄

First 4 sts ◄

► Last 14 sts

31 sts on a holder; keeping continuity, work next 51 sts in patt and place these sts on a holder for back neck; k1; *k2tog, k1; rep from * to end of row and place these 31 sts on a holder.

LEFT SHOULDER STRAP

Place left front and left back shoulder sts on 2 separate double-pointed needles *or* on 1 circular 3mm (US 3) needle. (**Note:** For circular needle, place sts so that both pointed ends are at neck edge.) With WS facing and a contrasting yarn, using 'thumb method', cast on 17 sts onto neck end of needle holding left back shoulder sts, then turn.

*Foundation row 1 (RS): With neck end of needle holding left front shoulder sts and using contrasting yarn, k across 17 cast-on sts; turn.
Break off contrasting yarn.
Foundation row 2: Join in main yarn and p across first 16 sts of strap; then p last st of strap tog with first st from front shoulder; turn.
Set chart patt on next row as follows—
Next row (RS): Sl 1 knitwise; p2; work 11 sts of zigzag panel (5th-15th sts of chart) following chart row 1; p2; ssk last st of strap tog with first st from back shoulder; turn.
Next row: With yarn at front, sl 1 purlwise; k2; work 11 zigzag panel sts

KEY

▯ k on RS rows; p on WS rows.

▬ p on RS rows; k on WS rows.

*T*he vertical patterns of Fife – worked entirely in knit and purl stitches – are typically Scottish. The tough double cast-on, gussets, half stocking-stitch sleeves and double cast-offs ensure that this gansey is designed to cope with all the rough and tumble of childhood.

from chart as set; k2; p last st of strap tog with next st from front shoulder; turn.
Next row: Sl 1 knitwise; p2; work 11 sts from chart as set; p2; ssk last st of strap tog with next st from back shoulder; turn.
Rep these last 2 rows until all shoulder sts have been incorporated into shoulder strap, so ending with chart row 21.
Break off yarn and place 17 strap sts on a holder.★★

RIGHT SHOULDER STRAP

Place right front and right back shoulder sts on needles as for left shoulder strap.
With WS facing and a contrasting yarn, using 'thumb method', cast on 17 sts on neck end of needle holding right front shoulder sts, then turn.
Work as left shoulder strap from ★ to ★★, but reading 'front shoulder' for 'back shoulder' and vice versa.

NECKBAND

Remove contrasting yarn from shoulder straps and place 17 loops formed by first row of main yarn on 2 holders.
With RS facing and 2¾mm (US 2) needles, beg at back neck st holder and pick up sts as follows—
(K1; k2tog; k45; k2tog; k1) all from back neck holder; k 17 sts from left shoulder strap holder; pick up and k 15 sts evenly down left side of front neck; k 23 sts from front neck holder; pick up and k 15 sts evenly up right side of front neck; k 17 sts from right shoulder strap holder to complete rnd. 136 sts.
Place a st marker on RH needle to mark beg of rnd and working in rnds, work k2, p2 rib for 5cm (2in), slipping marker on each rnd.
With yarn doubled, cast off knitwise.

SLEEVES

With RS facing and 3mm (US 3) needles, k 17 sts from gusset holder; pick up and k 54 sts evenly up armhole edge to shoulder strap; work sts from shoulder strap as follows—
K1; p2; keeping continuity, work chart rnd 2 of zigzag panel across next 11 sts;

p2; k1; pick up and k 54 sts evenly down armhole edge to complete rnd. 142 sts.
Shape Gusset
Place a st marker on RH needle to mark beg of rnd and working in rnds, beg shaping gusset and set sleeve patt as follows—
Next rnd: Ssk; k13; k2tog; p2; following chart rnd 3, beg at 30th st of 42-st rep and work last 13 sts of rep; rep 42 patt sts twice; work first 24 sts of rep; p2.
Cont in patt as set and working gusset sts in st st throughout, dec 1 st at each side of gusset (inside rev st st border) on every foll 4th rnd until 3 gusset sts in st st rem. 128 sts.
Work 3 rnds in patt without shaping.

Next rnd: K2; p2tog; p1; work 121 sts in patt as set; p1; slip next st (p st) onto RH needle, remove st marker and slip the slipped st back onto LH needle, then p2tog; place st marker on RH needle to mark next st (centre sleeve st) as beg of rnd.
Next rnd: P3; work 121 sts in patt; p2. Rep last rnd twice more.
Shape Lower Sleeve
Next rnd: P1; p2tog; work 121 sts in patt; p2tog.
Next rnd: P2; work 121 sts in patt; p1. Rep last rnd twice more.
Next rnd: P1 (seam st); k2tog; work 119 sts in patt; ssk. 122 sts.
Next rnd: P seam st; work rem sts in patt.

Rep last rnd twice more.

Next rnd: P seam st; k2tog; work in patt as set to last 2 sts; ssk.

Keeping continuity of patt and cont to p seam st throughout, work 3 rnds without shaping.

Dec 1 st at each side of seam st on next and every foll 4th rnd until 110 sts rem. Work 3 rnds without shaping.

Next rnd: P seam st; k2tog; k6; *k2tog, k8; rep from * to last 11 sts; k2tog; k7; k2tog. 98 sts rem.

P 2 rnds.

Next rnd: P seam st; k97.

Cont in this manner in st st (except for seam st) and dec 1 st at each side of seam st on next and every foll 4th rnd until 80 sts rem, then on every foll 3rd rnd until 68 sts rem.

Work in st st without shaping until sleeve measures 31cm (12¼in).

Cuff

Dec rnd: *K2tog, k4; rep from * to last 2 sts, k2tog. 56 sts.

Change to 2¾mm (US 2) needles and work k2, p2 rib for 5cm (2in).

With yarn doubled (as for cast-on for body), cast off knitwise.

FINISHING

Darn in loose ends. Either rinse, short spin and dry garment on a woolly board (see page 124), or turn garment wrong side out and press lightly, omitting ribs.

T̲he practical knitting features that make the fisher gansey Fife hard wearing also add to the beauty of the garment. With good washing care, Fife is sure to delight both wearers and observers for several generations.

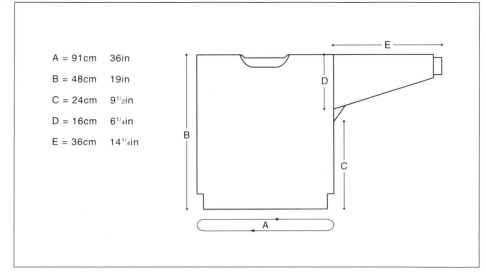

A = 91cm   36in

B = 48cm   19in

C = 24cm   9½in

D = 16cm   6¼in

E = 36cm   14¼in

ENGLAND

Traditional English fisher gansey style and pattern
were pared down to their essence, and when
well executed, these knitted garments had a simple
elegance of their own.

CORNWALL

SIZES

To fit small [medium, large]
Directions for larger sizes are given in brackets.
Where there is only one set of figures, it applies
to all sizes.

KNITTED
MEASUREMENTS

Underarm, excluding gussets
111.5[116.5,121.5]cm (44½[46½,48½]in)
Length 63[65,67]cm (24½[25½,26¼]in)
Sleeve length 45[47,49]cm
(17¾[18½,19¼]in)

MATERIALS

Yarn weight used: double knitting wool
(US knitting worsted)
13[14,15] x 50g (1¾oz) balls of Rowan
Designer DK in shade no. 658 Dark Sea
Green
1 set of double-pointed *or* circular 3¼mm
(US 3) and 4mm (US 6) needles
A 4½mm (US 7) needle of any type
4 stitch holders
Stitch markers

TENSION (GAUGE)

24 sts and 30 rows to 10cm (4in)
measured over st st, using 4mm (US 6)
needles

BODY

Body is worked in one piece to armhole.
With 3¼mm (US 3) needles, cast on
248[258,266] sts.
Place a st marker on RH needle to mark
beg of rnd, then making sure cast-on edge
is not twisted and working in rnds (RS
always facing), work k1, p1 rib for
7[8,8]cm (2¾[3,3]in), slipping marker on
each rnd.
Inc rnd: Keeping marker in place to
mark first st for beg of rnd and underarm
seam st, *p1 (seam st); k3[4,6]; (m1,
k13[12,10]) 9[10,12] times; m1; k3[4,6]*;
place a st marker on RH needle to mark
next st for centre of rnd and underarm
seam st, rep from * to * once more.
268[280,292] sts.
Change to 4mm (US 6) needles and

*T*he beauty of Cornwall *lies in*
its elegance of style and the
strength of contrast between the
smooth stocking-stitch areas and the
densely ribbed yoke. The patterned
neckband adds a contemporary touch
to an otherwise traditional English
gansey. The yoke is worked in
fisherman's rib pattern, which
produces a thick soft fabric that is
perfect for keeping chill winds at bay.

slipping markers on every rnd throughout,
set patt as follows—
Next rnd: *P seam st; k133[139,145]; rep
from * once more.
Rep last rnd until body measures
32[33,34]cm (12½[13,13¼]in) from beg.
Begin Gussets and Yoke Pattern
Reading every chart rnd from right to
left, beg gussets and chart patt as follows—
Chart rnd 1: *M1; k seam st; m1; rep 4
patt sts of first rnd of chart 33[34,36]
times; work last 1[3,1] sts of chart as
indicated; rep from * once more. (The

seam st and inc sts form the gussets – there
are now 3 sts in each gusset.)
Cont in chart patt as set and working all
gusset sts in st st, inc 1 st at each side of
each gusset on every foll 3rd rnd until
there are 15 sts in each gusset and all 19
rnds of chart have been completed.
296[308,320] sts.
Dec on back and front on next rnd as
follows—
First Size Only
Next rnd: *K 15 gusset sts; k3; (k2tog,
k4) 21 times; k2tog; k2; rep from * once
more. 111 sts rem on each of front and
back yoke.
Second Size Only
Next rnd: *K 15 gusset sts; (k2tog, k4)
22 times; k2tog; k3; k2tog; rep from *
once more. 115 sts rem on each of front
and back yoke.
Third Size Only
Next rnd: *K 15 gusset sts; k3; (k2tog,
k4) 23 times; k2tog; k2; rep from * once
more. 121 sts rem on each of front and
back yoke.
All Sizes
Beg fisherman's rib over each yoke as
follows—
Rnd 1: (K 15 gusset sts; *p1; k into st
below next st; rep from * to last yoke st;
p1) twice.
Rnd 2: (M1; k15; m1; *p into st below
next st; k1; rep from * to last yoke st; p
into st below next st) twice. (There are
now 17 sts in each gusset.)
First Size Only
Work 1 rnd without shaping, working
gusset sts in st st and working patt rnd 1 of
fisherman's rib over each yoke.
Second Size Only
Work 2 rnds without shaping, working
gusset sts in st st and working patt rnds 1
and 2 of fisherman's rib over each yoke.
Keeping continuity of patt as set, inc 1 st
at each side of each gusset on next rnd, so
ending after working patt rnd 1 of
fisherman's rib on yokes.
Third Size Only
Work 2 rnds without shaping, working
gusset sts in st st and working rnds 1 and 2
of fisherman's rib over each yoke.
Keeping continuity of patt as set, inc 1 st

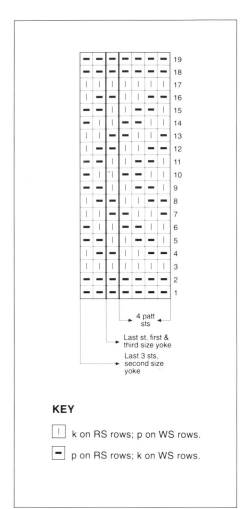

▬	▬	▬	▬	▬	▬		19
▬	▬	▬	▬	▬	▬		18
I	I	I	I	I	I		17
I	▬	▬	I	I	▬		16
▬	I	I	▬	▬	I		15
I	▬	I	I	I	I		14
I	I	I	I	I	I		13
I	▬	I	I	▬	I		12
▬	I	I	▬	▬	I		11
▬	I	I	▬	▬	I		10
I	▬	I	I	▬	I		9
I	▬	▬	I	I	▬		8
I	I	▬	I	I	▬		7
▬	I	I	▬	▬	I		6
▬	I	I	▬	▬	I		5
I	▬	▬	I	I	▬		4
I	I	I	I	I	I		3
▬	▬	▬	▬	▬	▬		2
▬	▬	▬	▬	▬	▬		1

← 4 patt → sts

→ Last st, first & third size yoke

→ Last 3 sts, second size yoke

KEY

| I | k on RS rows; p on WS rows.

| ▬ | p on RS rows; k on WS rows.

at each side of each gusset on next row and foll 3rd row, then work 1 rnd without shaping, so ending after working patt rnd 1 of fisherman's rib on yokes.

All Sizes

There are now 17[19,21] sts in each gusset.

Divide for Yokes

Place first 17[19,21] sts of rnd (gusset) on a holder, leave next 111[115,121] sts (front yoke sts) on a spare needle, place next 17[19,21] sts (gusset) on a holder. 111[115,121] sts of back yoke rem.

Back Yoke

Beg with a WS row and working back and forth in rows (instead of working in rnds), cont working in fisherman's rib over 111[115,121] sts of back yoke as follows—

Row 1 (WS): *K into st below next st;

p1; rep from * to last st; k into st below next st.

Row 2: *P1; k into st below next st; rep from * to last st; p1.

Rep these 2 rows until yoke measures 21[21.5,22]cm (8¼[8½,8¾]in) from top of gussets, ending with RS facing for next row.

Shape Back Neck

Next row (RS): Keeping continuity, work 42[43,45] sts in patt; place next 27[29,31] sts on a holder for back neck; turn, leaving rem sts on a spare needle. Keeping continuity of patt throughout, shape right side of neck as follows—
***Dec 1 st at neck edge on next and every foll alt row 4 times in all. 38[39,41] sts rem.

Work without shaping until yoke measures 23[23.5,24]cm (9[9¼,9½]in) from top of gussets.

Place sts on a spare needle.***

With RS facing, rejoin yarn to 42[43,45] sts of left side of neck, and keeping continuity, shape as right side of neck from *** to ***.

Front Yoke

With WS facing, rejoin yarn to 111[115,121] sts of front yoke and working back and forth in rows, work in fisherman's rib as back yoke until front yoke measures 15[15.5,15.5]cm (6[6¼,6¼]in) from top of gusset, ending with RS facing for next row.

Shape Front Neck

Next row (RS): Keeping continuity, work 49[50,52] sts in patt; place next 13[15,17] sts on a holder for front neck; turn, leaving rem sts on a spare needle. Keeping continuity of patt throughout, shape left side of neck as follows—
****Dec 1 st at neck edge on every foll row twice, then at same edge on every foll alt row 4 times, then on every foll 3rd row 5 times. 38[39,41] sts rem.

Work without shaping until there are same number of rows as back to shoulder. Place sts on a spare needle.****

With RS facing, rejoin yarn to 49[50,52] sts of right side of neck and keeping continuity, shape as left side of neck from **** to ****.

NECKBAND

Before beg neckband, join back and front at shoulders as follows—

With 4½mm (US 7) needle, holding WS of back and front tog and with RS of back facing, cast off shoulder sts tog. (See page 121 for casting off sts tog.)

Begin Neckband

With RS facing and 4mm (US 6) needles, beg at back neck st holder and pick up sts as follows—

From back neck holder — k1[2,1]; (m1, k3[3,4]) 8[8,7] times; m1; k2[3,2]; there are now 36[38,39] sts on needle; pick up and k 6 sts up left side of back neck and 25[25,26] sts evenly down left side of front neck to front neck holder; from front neck holder — k1[2,1]; (m1, k3[3,5]) 4[4,3] times; m1; k0[1,1]; there are now 85[89,92] sts on needle; pick up and k 25[25,26] sts evenly up right side of front neck and 6 sts down right side of back neck to complete rnd. 116[120,124] sts.

Place a st marker on RH needle to mark beg of rnd and working in rnds, beg at chart rnd 1 and work 19 rnds of chart patt, rep 4 patt sts 29[30,31] times in each rnd.

Work 15 rnds in st st.

Cast off loosely and evenly.

Turn neckband to inside at last rnd of chart patt and catch stitch cast-off edge around neckline.

SLEEVES

With RS facing and 4mm (US 6) needles, k 17[19,21] sts from gusset holder; pick up and k 93[95,97] sts evenly around armhole edge to complete rnd. 110[114,118] sts.

Shape Gusset

Place a st marker on RH needle to mark beg of rnd and working in rnds, beg shaping gusset and working fisherman's rib as follows—

Next rnd: Ssk; k13[15,17]; k2tog; *p1; k into st below next st; rep from * to last st of rnd; p1.

Next rnd: K 15[17,19] gusset sts; *p into st below next st; k1; rep from * to last st of rnd; p into st below next st.

Cont in patt as set, working rib on sleeve

sts and working gusset sts in st st, and work 1 row more without shaping, then dec 1 st at each side of gusset on next and every foll 3rd rnd until 5[7,9] sts rem in gusset and 16 rnds in fisherman's rib have been worked in all. 98[102,106] sts. Inc on next rnd as follows—

Next rnd: K 5[7,9] gusset sts; k4[5,6]; *m1; k5; rep from * to last 4[5,6] sts of rnd; m1; k4[5,6]. There are now 111[113,115] sleeve sts and 116[120,124] sts in total.

Beg chart patt from rnd 1, set sleeve patt as follows—

Chart rnd 1: K 5[7,9] gusset sts; rep 4 patt sts of first rnd of chart 27[28,28] times; work last 3[1,3] sts of chart as indicated.

Cont in patt as set, working chart patt on sleeve sts and working gusset sts in st st, until 19 rnds of chart have been completed, then work sleeve sts in st st, AND AT THE SAME TIME shape gussets as follows—

Dec 1 st at each side of gusset on next rnd (chart rnd 2) and every foll 3rd rnd until 3 gusset sts in st st rem. 114[116,118] sts. Work 2 rnds in patt as set without shaping.

Next rnd: Sl 1-k2tog-psso; work in patt to end of rnd.

Next rnd: P1 (seam st); work in patt to end of rnd.

Cont to p seam st to cuff, work 2 rnds in patt as set without shaping.

Shape Lower Sleeve

Keeping continuity of chart patt as set, beg shaping lower sleeve as follows—

Next rnd: P1 (seam st); k2tog; work in patt to last 2 sts; ssk.

Cont to p seam st to cuff, work 3 rnds in patt as set without shaping.

Keeping continuity of patt as set (changing to st st for sleeve sts when chart has been completed), dec 1 st at each side of seam st on next and every foll 4th rnd until 70 sts rem, then on every foll 3rd rnd until 64[66,68] sts rem.

Work as set without shaping until sleeve measures 38[40,42]cm (15[15¾,16½]in).

Cuff

Dec rnd: (K2tog, k5) 2[3,4] times; (k2tog, k4) 6[4,2] times; (k2tog, k5) 2[3,4] times. 54[56,58] sts. Change to 3¼mm (US 3) needles and work k1, p1 rib for 7cm (2¾in). Cast off in rib.

FINISHING

Darn in loose ends. Either rinse, short spin and dry garment on a woolly board (see page 124), or turn garment wrong side out and press all st st areas lightly, omitting ribs and chart pattern areas. Press inside of neckband lightly on WS.

The pattern stitches used for my Cornwall design are very simple to work, although fisherman's rib is a little slow to knit because it is so dense. The result is well worth the effort, as this is a classic sweater which combines easy style and warm practicality.

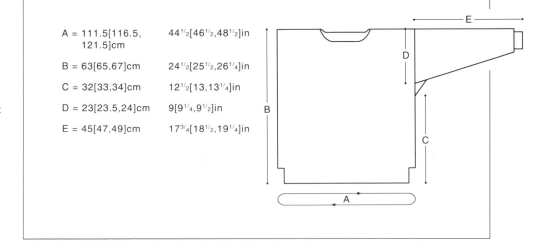

A = 111.5[116.5, 121.5]cm	44½[46½,48½]in
B = 63[65,67]cm	24½[25½,26¼]in
C = 32[33,34]cm	12½[13,13¼]in
D = 23[23.5,24]cm	9[9¼,9½]in
E = 45[47,49]cm	17¾[18½,19¼]in

NORFOLK

SIZES
To fit small [medium, large, extra large]
*Directions for larger sizes are given in brackets.
Where there is only one set of figures, it applies
to all sizes.*

KNITTED
MEASUREMENTS
Underarm, excluding gussets
97.5[105.5,113.5,122.5]cm (39[42,45¼,
49]in)
Length 61[63.5,66,69]cm (24[25,26,27]in)
Sleeve length 43[46,48,51]cm
(17[18,19,20]in)

MATERIALS
Yarn weight used: 4-ply wool and
cotton (US sport)
12[13,14,15] x 50g (1¾oz) balls of Rowan
Wool and Cotton in shade no. 911 'Dove'
1 set of double-pointed *or* circular 2¾mm
(US 1) and 3mm (US 2) needles
A 3¼mm (US 3) needle of any type
7 stitch holders
Stitch markers

TENSION (GAUGE)
15 sts and 19 rows to 5cm (2in) measured
over st st, using 3mm (US 2) needles

BODY
Body is worked in one piece to armhole.
With 2¾mm (US 1) needles, cast on
272[292,312,336] sts.
Place a st marker on RH needle to mark
beg of rnd, then making sure cast-on edge
is not twisted and working in rnds (RS
always facing), work k2, p2 rib for
6[7,7,8]cm (2½[2¾,2¾,3]in), slipping
marker on each rnd.
First Size Only
Inc rnd: ★(M1, k14) 3 times; (m1, k13) 4
times; (m1, k14) 3 times; rep from ★ once
more. 292 sts.
Second Size Only
Inc rnd: ★M1; k13; (m1, k12) 10 times;
m1; k13; rep from ★ once more. 316 sts.
Third Size Only
Inc rnd: ★M1; k12; (m1, k11) 12 times;
m1; k12; rep from ★ once more. 340 sts.

*S*ome of the loveliest knit and purl
patterns come from the Norfolk
coast and were traditionally used on
the back and front yokes of plain
ganseys. I have stayed true to this
format in Norfolk, as the delicate
lines and shapes of the pattern are
best displayed against plain stocking
stitch and simple styling. I have
deviated from the tradition only
slightly by extending the pattern to
the sleeve tops.

Fourth Size Only
Inc rnd: ★M1; k10; m1; k11; rep from ★
to end of rnd. 368 sts.
All Sizes
Change to 3mm (US 2) needles and set
patt as follows—
Rnd 1: Keeping marker in place to mark
first st for beg of rnd and underarm seam
st, p1 (seam st); k 145[157,169,183] sts
(front); place a st marker on RH needle to
mark next st for centre of rnd and
underarm seam st, p1 (seam st); k
145[157,169,183] sts (back).

Rep last rnd until body measures
25[25,25.5,25.5]cm (9¾[9¾,10,10]in) from
inc rnd, slipping markers on every rnd
throughout.
Begin Gussets and Yoke Pattern
Beg gussets and chart A yoke patt as
follows—
Chart rnd 1: Slip marker, m1; k1 (seam
st); m1; p first rnd of chart A over
145[157,169,183] sts of front; slip marker,
m1; k1 (seam st); m1; p first rnd of chart
A over 145[157,169,183] sts of back. (The
seam st and inc sts form the gussets – there
are now 3 sts in each gusset.)
Cont working chart A patt as set over
front and back sts, and working all gusset
sts in st st, inc 1 st at at each side of each
gusset on every foll 4th rnd until chart rnd
11 has been completed. (There are now
7 sts in each gusset.)
Reading every chart rnd from right to
left, set remaining chart patt as follows—
Chart rnd 12: ★K 7 gusset sts; work first
7[0,6,0] sts of rnd 12 of chart A as
indicated; rep 26 patt sts 5[6,6,7] times;
work last 8[1,7,1] sts of chart as indicated;
rep from ★ once more.
Cont in patt as set, rep chart rnds 12
through 23 throughout, and cont to inc
1 st at each side of gusset on every foll 4th
rnd until there are 17[19,21,23] sts in each
gusset, so ending after working an odd-
numbered chart rnd. 324[352,380,412] sts.
Divide for Yokes
Place first 17[19,21,23] sts of rnd (gusset)
on a holder, leave next 145[157,169,183]
sts (front yoke sts) on a spare needle, place
next 17[19,21,23] sts (gusset) on a holder.
145[157,169,183] sts of back yoke rem.
Back Yoke
Beg with a WS row and keeping
continuity of patt, work 145[157,169,183]
sts of back yoke in patt, working back and
forth in rows (now reading WS chart
rows from left to right and RS rows from
right to left) until yoke measures
21.5[22,23,24]cm (8½[8¾,9¼,9½]in) from
top of gussets, ending with RS facing for
next row.
P 1 row. K 1 row.
Next row (RS): K43[48,52,58]; (k2tog,
k1) twice; place these last 47[52,56,62] sts

CHART A

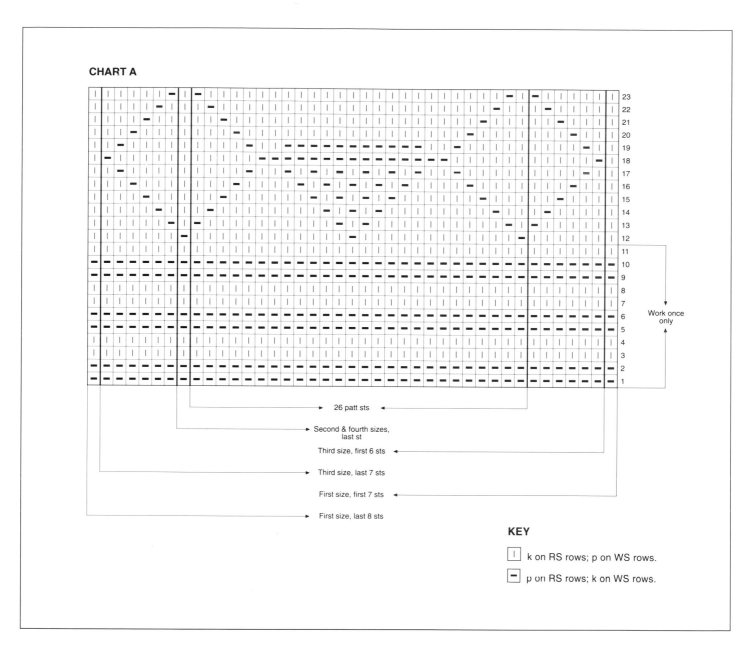

26 patt sts

Second & fourth sizes, last st

Third size, first 6 sts

Third size, last 7 sts

First size, first 7 sts

First size, last 8 sts

Work once only

KEY

| k on RS rows; p on WS rows.

− p on RS rows; k on WS rows.

on a holder; k next 47[49,53,55] sts and place these sts on a holder for back neck; (k1, k2tog) twice; k43[48,52,58]; place these last 47[52,56,62] sts on a spare needle.

Front Yoke

With WS facing, rejoin yarn to 145[157,169,183] sts of front yoke and keeping continuity, work in patt as set, working back and forth in rows until front yoke measures 18[18.5,19,19]cm (7[7¼,7½,7½]in) from top of gusset, ending with RS facing for next row.

Shape Front Neck

Next row (RS): Keeping continuity, work 56[61,66,72] sts in patt; place next 33[35,37,39] sts on a holder; turn, leaving rem sts on a spare needle.

Keeping continuity of patt throughout, shape left side of neck as follows—
**Dec 1 st at neck edge on every foll row 3 times, then at same edge on every foll alt row 4[4,5,5] times.
49[54,58,64] sts rem.

Work without shaping until there are same number of chart rows as back,

ending with RS facing for next row.
P 1 row. K 1 row.***

Next row (RS): K43[48,52,58]; (k2tog, k1) twice and place these 47[52,56,62] sts on a spare needle.

With RS facing, rejoin yarn to 56[61,66, 72] sts of right side of neck, and keeping continuity of patt, work 1 row without shaping, then shape as left side of neck from ** to ***.

Next row (RS): (K1, k2tog) twice; k43[48,52,58] and place these 47[52,56,62] sts on a holder.

CHART B

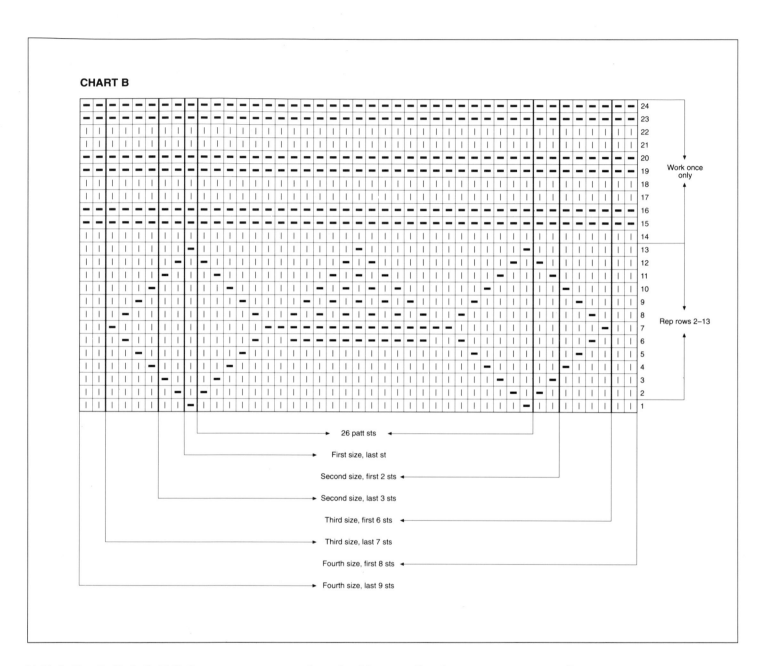

NECK GUSSETS

Before beg left neck gusset, join back and front at shoulder as follows—
Turn body wrong side out. With 3¼mm (US 3) needle, holding RS of left back and front shoulders tog and beg at armhole edge of shoulder, cast off back and front shoulder sts tog until **5** sts rem on each of front and back shoulder spare needles at neck edge. (See page 121 for casting off sts tog.) Do not break off yarn.

Left Neck Gusset

Turn body right side out and place single st rem from shoulder cast off on 3mm (US 2) needle.
With 3mm (US 2) needles and RS facing, work gusset as follows—

Row 1 (RS): With needle holding single st, k next st from front shoulder spare needle — there are now 2 sts on RH needle; turn.

Row 2: P2; p next st from back shoulder spare needle; turn.

Row 3: K3; k next st from front shoulder spare needle; turn.

Row 4: P4; p next st from back shoulder spare needle; turn.

Cont in this manner, working 6 rows more and incorporating all the rem sts from shoulders.
Place 11 gusset sts on a holder.

Right Neck Gusset

Turn body wrong side out. Place right back and front shoulder sts onto separate spare needles. With 3¼mm (US 3) needle, holding RS of right back and front shoulders tog and beg at armhole edge of shoulder, cast off back and front shoulder sts tog until 5 sts rem on each of front and back shoulder spare needles at neck edge. Do not break off yarn.

Work neck gusset as for left side of neck, but picking up sts from back shoulder on k rows of gusset, and front shoulder on p rows of gusset.

Place 11 gusset sts on a holder.

NECKBAND

With RS facing and 2¾mm (US 1) needles, k 47[49,53,55] sts from back neck holder; k 11 sts from left neck gusset holder; pick up and k 13[13,14,14] sts evenly down left side of front neck to front neck holder; k 33[35,37,39] sts from front neck holder; pick up and k 13[13,14,14] sts evenly up right side of front neck to right neck gusset; k 11 sts from right neck gusset holder to complete rnd. 128[132,140,144] sts.

Place a st marker on RH needle to mark beg of rnd and working in rnds, work k2, p2 rib for 6cm (2½in), slipping marker on each rnd.

Cast off knitwise.

SLEEVES

With RS facing and 3mm (US 2) needles, k 17[19,21,23] sts from gusset holder; pick up and k 131[135,143,147] sts evenly around armhole edge to complete rnd. 148[154,164,170] sts.

Shape Gusset

Place a st marker on RH needle to mark beg of rnd and working in rnds, beg shaping gusset as follows—

Next rnd: Ssk; k13[15,17,19]; k2tog; p131[135,143,147].

Next rnd: K 15[17,19,21] gusset sts; p131[135,143,147].

K 1 rnd.

Beg chart B from rnd 1, set sleeve patt as follows—

Chart rnd 1: K 15[17,19,21] gusset sts; work first 0[2,6,8] sts of chart B as indicated; rep 26 patt sts 5 times; work last 1[3,7,9] sts of chart as indicated.

Cont in patt as set, **rep rnds 2 through 13 of chart B 3 times in all, then work rnds 14 through 24 of chart B once only and thereafter work all rnds in st st***, AND AT THE SAME TIME shape gussets as follows—

Working chart patt as set, and working gusset sts in st st throughout, dec 1 st at each side of gusset on next rnd (chart rnd 2) and every foll 4th rnd until 3 gusset sts in st st rem. 134[138,146,150] sts.

Work 3 rnds in patt as set without shaping.

Next rnd: Sl 1-k2tog-psso; work in patt to end of rnd.

Next rnd: P1 (seam st); work in patt to end of rnd.

Cont to p seam st to cuff, work 2 rnds in patt as set without shaping.

Shape Lower Sleeve

Keeping continuity of patt as set, beg shaping lower sleeve as follows—

Next rnd: P1 (seam st); k2tog; work in patt to last 2 sts; ssk.

Work 3 rnds in patt as set without shaping.

Keeping continuity of patt as set (from ** to ***), dec 1 st at each side of seam st on next and every foll 4th rnd until 78[80,84,86] sts rem.

K 2 rnds without shaping.

Cuff

Shape for cuff as follows—

First Size Only

Dec rnd: (K2tog, k4) 4 times; (k2tog, k3) 6 times; (k2tog, k4) 4 times. 64 sts.

Second Size Only

Dec rnd: *K2tog, k3; rep from * to end of rnd. 64 sts.

Third Size Only

Dec rnd: (K2tog, k4) twice; (k2tog, k3) 12 times; (k2tog, k4) twice. 68 sts.

Fourth Size Only K2T K3

Dec rnd: K2tog; k5; (k2tog, k4) 12 times; k2tog; k5. 72 sts. K2T K5

All Sizes 56 stitches

Change to 2¾mm (US 1) needles and work k2, p2 rib until sleeve measures 43[46,48,51]cm (17[18,19,20]in).

Cast off knitwise.

FINISHING

Darn in loose ends. Either rinse, short spin and dry garment on a woolly board (see page 124 for information), or turn garment wrong side out and press all st st areas lightly, omitting ribs and chart pattern areas.

A = 97.5[105.5,113.5,122.5]cm   39[42,45¼,49]in

B = 61[63.5,66,69]cm   24[25,26,27]in

C = 31[32,32.5,33.5]cm   12¼[12½,12¾,13]in

D = 22.5[23,24,25]cm   8¾[9,9½,9¾]in

E = 43[46,48,51]cm   17[18,19,20]in

SCARBOROUGH

RATING ★ ★

SIZES
To fit approx age 4[6,8,10,12] years or
58[63,68,72,76]cm (23[25,27,28½,30]in)
chest
*Directions for larger sizes are given in brackets.
Where there is only one set of figures, it applies
to all sizes.*

KNITTED
MEASUREMENTS
Underarm, excluding gussets 66[70,75.5,
83.5,89]cm (26½[28,30,33¼,35½]in)
Length 39[42,45,48,51]cm (15¼[16½,17¾,
19,20]in)
Sleeve length 30[32.5,35,38,42.5]cm
(11¾[13,13¾,15,16½]in)

MATERIALS
Yarn weight used: 5-ply gansey wool
(US sport)
4[4,5,5,6] x 100g (3½oz) balls of Alice
Starmore's *Scottish Fleet* in Natural
1 set of double-pointed *or* circular 3mm
(US 3) needles
1 set of double-pointed 2¼mm (US 1)
needles
8 stitch holders
Stitch markers

TENSION (GAUGE)
15 sts and 19 rows to 5cm (2in) measured
over st st, using 3mm (US 3) needles

BODY
Back and front lower border flaps are
worked separately first, then they are
joined and body is worked in one piece to
armhole.
Border Flaps
With 2 double-pointed or circular 3mm
(US 3) needles, cast on 98[104,112,
124,132] sts.
Working back and forth in rows, work
first 6 rows of lower border as follows—
P 1 row (RS); k 2 rows; p 2 rows;
k 1 row.
Work patt as follows—
Row 1 (RS): K6[7,7,7,7]; *p2, k2;
rep from * to last 8[9,9,9,9] sts; p2;
k6[7,7,7,7].

*T*here are many old photographs
in museums and private
collections that testify that small
children – as well as men and boys –
were beneficiaries of the skills of
gansey knitters. Children's ganseys
were generally styled like the basic
working ganseys, no doubt for the
sake of ease and speed of knitting.
Scarborough *demonstrates the charm
of simplicity and is modelled on a
working gansey from the Yorkshire
town it is named after.*

Rows 2 and 3: P6[7,7,7,7], *k2, p2,
rep from * to last 8[9,9,9,9] sts; k2;
p6[7,7,7,7].
Rows 4: As row 1.
Rep these 4 rows and work 10[10,
14,14,14] rows in total, so ending after

working patt row 2 with RS facing for
next row.
P 1 row (RS); k 2 rows; p 2 rows; k 1
row, so ending with RS facing for next
row.
Break off yarn and leave border flap sts on
a spare needle.
Work a second identical border flap, but
do not break off yarn.
Join Border Flaps
With RS facing, k across sts of second
border flap; cast on 1 st on RH needle;
with RS of first border facing, k across all
sts of first border flap; cast on 1 st.
198[210,226,250,266] sts.
With RS still facing and set of double-
pointed or circular 3mm (US 3) needles,
join borders into a circle and work first
rnd as follows—
Rnd 1: K 98[104,112,124,132] sts (back);
place a st marker on RH needle to mark
next st for centre of rnd and underarm
seam st, p next st (the cast-on st); k
98[104,112,124,132] sts (front); place st
marker on RH needle to mark next st
(the cast-on st) for beg of rnd and
underarm seam st.
Working in rnds (RS always facing) and
keeping markers in place on every rnd
throughout, work next rnd as follows—
Rnd 2: P1 (seam st); k 98[104,112,
124,132] back sts; p1 (seam st); k 98[104,
112,124,132] front sts.
Rep last rnd until body measures
12[13.5,13.5,14,14]cm (4¾[5¼,5¼,5½,
5½]in) from beg of st st rnds.
Begin Yoke Border
Beg yoke border as follows—
★★Next rnd: *P seam st; k1; p96[102,
110,122,130]; k1; rep from * once more.
Rep last rnd once more.★★
Next rnd: *P seam st; k98[104,112,124,
132]; rep from * once more.
Rep last rnd once more.
Rep from ★★ to ★★ once.
Begin Gussets and Main Yoke Patt
Rnd 1: M1, k seam st, m1 (these 3 sts beg
first gusset); k6[7,7,7,7]; *p2, k2; rep from
* to within 8[9,9,9,9] sts of next seam st;
p2; k6[7,7,7,7] (these last 98[104,112,
124,132] sts are back yoke); m1; k seam
st; m1 (these last 3 sts beg second gusset);

*T*he tunic style of this gansey has a patterned border with side slits. The yoke features a textured check pattern and ridge-patterned armhole borders. Easy to knit and to wear, Scarborough comes in five sizes. Knitted here in 5-ply gansey wool, it would also look lovely in a smooth wool and cotton mix.

k6[7,7,7,7]; *p2, k2; rep from * to within 8[9,9,9,9] sts of end of rnd; p2; k6[7,7,7,7] (these last 98[104,112,124, 132] sts are front yoke).

Rnd 2: K 3 gusset sts; k the k sts and p the p sts on back yoke as previous rnd; k 3 gusset sts; k the k sts and p the p sts on front yoke as previous rnd.

Rnd 3: K 3 gusset sts; k1; p5[6,6,6,6]; *k2, p2; rep from * to within 8[9,9,9,9] sts of second gusset; k2; p5[6,6,6,6]; k1; k 3 gusset sts; k1; p5[6,6,6,6]; *k2, p2; rep from * to within 8[9,9,9,9] sts of end of rnd; k2; p5[6,6,6,6]; k1.

Rnd 4: As rnd 3.

Cont in this manner, rep last 4 patt rnds over back and front yoke sts, inc 1 st at each side of each gusset on next and every foll 4th rnd, working all increased gusset sts in st st, until there are 13[15,15,17,19] sts in each gusset, ending after working an odd-numbered patt rnd. 222[238,254,282,302] sts.

Divide for Yokes

Place first 13[15,15,17,19] sts of rnd (gusset) on a holder, leave next 98[104, 112,124,132] sts (back yoke sts) on a spare needle, place next 13[15,15,17,19] sts (gusset) on a holder. 98[104,112,124,132] sts of front yoke rem.

Front Yoke

Beg with a WS row and keeping continuity of main yoke patt, work 98[104,112,124,132] sts of front yoke back and forth in rows until front yoke measures 9.5[10,12,13,14]cm (3¾[4,4¾, 5,5½]in) from top of gusset, ending with RS facing for next row.

Shape Front Neck

Next row (RS): Keeping continuity, work 41[43,46,51,54] sts in patt; place next 16[18,20,22,24] sts on a holder; turn, leaving rem sts on a spare needle. Keeping continuity of patt throughout, shape left side of neck as follows—
***Work 1 row without shaping.

Next row: Work in patt to last 3 sts and place these 3 sts on a holder.
Work 1 row without shaping.

Next row: Work in patt to last 2 sts and place these 2 sts on a holder.
Dec 1 st at neck edge on every foll row 4 times, then at same edge on every foll alt row 3[3,3,4,4] times.
29[31,34,38,41] sts rem.
Change to garter st and cont to dec at neck edge on alt rows 2[2,3,2,2] times more. 27[29,31,36,39] sts rem.
Work 4[6,4,6,6] rows in garter st without shaping.
Place sts on a spare needle.***
With RS facing, rejoin yarn to 41[43, 46,51,54] sts of right side of neck and keeping continuity, shape as left side of neck from *** to ***, but work 1 row without shaping after dec before changing to garter st.

Back Yoke

With WS facing, rejoin yarn to 98[104,112,124,132] sts of back yoke and keeping continuity of patt, work back and forth in rows until yoke measures same as front to garter st, ending with WS facing for next row.

Shape Back Neck

Next row (WS): K29[32,35,40,43]; place next 40[40,42,44,46] sts on a holder for back neck; turn, leaving rem sts on a spare needle.

Shape left side of neck as follows—

★★★★Working in garter st (k every row), dec 1 st at neck edge of next and every foll alt row 2[3,4,4,4] times in all. 27[29,31,36,39] sts rem.

Work 4[4,2,2,2] rows in garter st without shaping.

Place sts on a spare needle.★★★★

With WS facing, rejoin yarn to 29[32,35,40,43] sts of right side of neck and shape as left side of back neck from ★★★★ to ★★★★.

SLEEVES

Before beg sleeves, join back and front at shoulders as follows—

Turn body inside out, then with 3mm (US 3) needles, holding RS of back and front tog and beg at armhole edge cast off shoulder sts tog. (See page 121.)

Begin Sleeve

With RS facing and 3mm (US 3) needles, k 13[15,15,17,19] sts from gusset holder; working into plain st at armhole edge, pick up and k 91[99,109,117,125] sts evenly around armhole edge to complete rnd. 104[114,124,134,144] sts.

Shape Gusset

Place a st marker on RH needle to mark beg of rnd and working in rnds, beg shaping gusset as follows—

Next rnd: Ssk; k9[11,11,13,15]; k2tog; k91[99,109,117,125].

K 3 rnds without shaping.

Next rnd: Ssk; k7[9,9,11,13]; k2tog; k91[99,109,117,125].

K 3 rnds without shaping.

Cont in this manner, working in st st and dec 1 st at each side of gusset on next and every foll 4th rnd until 3 gusset sts rem. 94[102,112,120,128] sts.

K 3 rnds without shaping.

Next rnd: Sl 1-k2tog-psso; k to end of rnd.

Next rnd: P1 (seam st); k to end of rnd. Cont to p seam st to cuff, k 2 rnds without shaping.

Shape Lower Sleeve

Beg shaping lower sleeve as follows—

Next rnd: P1 (seam st); k2tog, work in patt to last 2 sts; ssk.

K 3 rnds without shaping.

Cont in st st to cuff, dec 1 st at each side of seam st on next and every foll 4th rnd until 54[58,80,84,88] sts rem, then on every foll 3rd rnd 0[0,9,9,9] times in all. 54[58,62,66,70] sts rem.

Work without shaping until sleeve measures 27[29.5,31,34,37.5]cm (10½[11¾,12¼,13½,14¾]in).

Cuff

First and Fourth Sizes Only

Dec rnd: ★K2tog; k7[9]; rep from ★ 6 times. 48[60] sts.

Second, Third and Fifth Sizes Only

Dec rnd: ★(K2tog, k8[9,10]) 2[1,2] times★; (k2tog, k7[8,9]) 2[4,2] times; rep from ★ to ★ once. 52[56,64] sts.

All Sizes

Change to 2¼mm (US 1) needles and work k2, p2 rib for 3[3,4,4,4.5]cm (1¼[1¼,1½,1½,1¾]in). Cast off knitwise.

NECKBAND

With RS facing and 2¼mm (US 1) needles, k 40[40,42,44,46] sts from back neck holder; pick up and k 6[8,8,8,8] sts up left side of back neck and 17[20,20, 22,22] sts evenly down left side of front neck to first front neck holder; k 26[28, 30,32,34] sts from all front neck holders; pick up and k 17[20,20,22,22] sts evenly up right side of front neck and 6[8,8,8,8] sts down right side of back neck to complete rnd. 112[124,128,136,140] sts. Place a st marker on RH needle to mark beg of rnd and working in rnds, work k2, p2 rib for 3[3,4,4,4.5]cm (1¼[1¼,1½,1½, 1¾]in). Cast off knitwise.

FINISHING

Darn in loose ends. Either rinse, short spin and dry garment on a woolly board (see page 124), or turn garment wrong side out and press all st st areas lightly, omitting ribs and patterned areas.

A = 66[70,75.5,83.5,89]cm   26½[28,30,33¼,35½]in

B = 39[42,45,48,51]cm   15¼[16½,17¾,19,20]in

C = 17.5[19,20,20.5,20.5]cm   7[7½,8,8¼,8¼]in

D = 15[16.5,18,19.5,20.5]cm   6[6½,7¼,7¾,8¼]in

E = 30[32.5,35,38,42.5]cm   11¾[13,13¾,15,16½]in

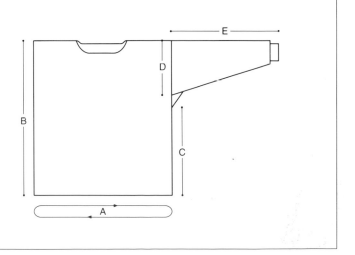

FILEY

SIZES

To fit small [medium, large, extra large]
Directions for larger sizes are given in brackets. Where there is only one set of figures, it applies to all sizes.

KNITTED MEASUREMENTS

Underarm 113[119,126,132]cm (45[47½, 50,53]in)
Length 77.5[80,82,84]cm (30½[31½,32¼, 33]in)
Sleeve length 53[54,55,56]cm (21[21¼, 21¾,22]in)

WASHED MEASUREMENTS

Underarm 113[119,126,132]cm (45[47½, 50,53]in)
Length 65[67.5,69.5,71.5]cm (25½[26½, 27¼,28]in)
Sleeve length 45[46,47,48]cm (17¾[18, 18½,18¾]in)

MATERIALS

Yarn weight used: indigo dyed unshrunk double knitting cotton (US medium weight cotton)
22[23,24,25] x 50g (1¾oz) balls of Rowan *Den-m-nit Cotton DK* in shade no. 225 'Nashville'
1 pair each 3¼mm (US 3) and 3¾mm (US 5) needles
1 set of double-pointed *or* short circular 3¼mm (US 3) needles
1 cable needle
6 stitch holders
Stitch markers

TENSION (GAUGE)

22 sts and 30 rows to 10cm (4in) measured over st st (before washing), using 3¾mm (US 5) needles

SPECIAL NOTE

Rowan *Den-m-nit Indigo Dyed Cotton DK* will shrink and fade when washed. When washed for the first time the yarn will shrink by up to one fifth in length, but the width with remain the same. This

*T*he most elaborately patterned English ganseys were to be found in the Yorkshire town of Filey. This was an important port of call for Scottish herring lassies, and the influence of these young women on the Filey knitters' work is manifest in the use of vertical panel patterns. The Filey knitters were particularly fond of combining rope cables with diamond and simple-textured panels.

sweater is specially designed for this yarn and all the necessary adjustments have been made in the instructions to obtain the washed measurements listed above.

BACK

**With 3¼mm (US 3) needles, cast on 122[128,134,142] sts.
Work k1, p1 rib for 8cm (3in).
Inc rnd (WS): Keeping continuity of rib, rib 7[4,1,5]; *m1, rib 6; rep from * to last 7[4,1,5] sts; m1; rib 7[4,1,5].
141[149,157,165] sts.
Change to 3¾mm (US 5) needles and

reading chart A (page 52) from right to left for RS (odd-numbered) rows and from left to right for WS (even-numbered) rows, set patt as follows—
Chart row 1 (RS): Work first 2[6,10,14] sts of row 1 of chart A as indicated; rep 41 patt sts 3 times; work last 16[20,24,28] sts of chart as indicated.
Chart row 2: Work first 16[20,24,28] sts of row 2 of chart A as indicated; rep 41 patt sts 3 times; work last 2[6,10,14] sts of chart as indicated.
Cont in chart patt as set, rep 12 patt rows until back measures 69[71.5,73,75]cm (27[28¼,28¾,29½]in) from beg, ending with WS facing for next row.
Dec row (WS): P6[10,14,18]; (p2tog, p2, p2tog, p35) 3 times; p2tog; p2; p2tog; p6[10,14,18].
133[141,149,157] sts rem.**
Work Rig and Furrow patt as follows—
Row 1 (RS): Purl.
Row 2: Knit.
Row 3: Knit.
Row 4: Purl.
Rep 4 patt rows 5 times in all.
Third and Fourth Sizes Only
Work patt rows 1 and 2 once more.
All Sizes: Shape Back Neck
Next row (RS): Keeping continuity of Rig and Furrow patt, work 50[54,57,61] sts in patt; place next 33[33,35,35] sts on a holder for back neck; turn, leaving rem sts on a spare needle.
Keeping continuity of Rig and Furrow patt throughout, shape right side of neck as follows—
***Cast off 3 sts at beg of next row.
Dec 1 st at neck edge on next 2 rows.
Place rem 45[49,52,56] sts on a holder.***
With RS facing, rejoin yarn to sts of left side of neck, and work 2 rows without shaping, then shape as right side of neck from *** to ***.

FRONT

Work as back from ** to **.
Shape Front Neck
Working in Rig and Furrow patt as back and keeping continuity throughout, divide for neck as follows—

Next row (RS): Work 60[64,67,71] sts in patt; place next 13[13,15,15] sts on a holder for front neck; turn, leaving rem sts on a spare needle.

Shape left side of neck as follows—
★★★Cast off 3 sts at beg of next row.
Work 1 row without shaping.
Cast off 2 sts at beg of next row.
Dec 1 st at neck edge on every foll row 4 times, then at same edge on every foll alt row 6 times. 45[49,52,56] sts rem.
Work without shaping until there are same number of rows as back in Rig and Furrow patt, ending at armhole edge. Place sts on a holder.★★★
With RS facing, rejoin yarn to sts of right side of neck, and work 2 rows without shaping, then shape as left side of front neck from ★★★ to ★★★.

COLLAR
Before beg collar, join back and front at shoulders as follows—
With 3¾mm (US 5) needles, holding RS of back and front tog, cast off shoulder sts tog. (See page 121 for casting off sts tog.)
Begin Collar
With RS facing and double-pointed or circular 3¾mm (US 3) needles, beg at back neck and k 33[33,35,35] sts from back neck holder; pick up and k 30[30,31,31] sts evenly up left back neck and down left side of front neck to front neck holder; k 13[13,15,15] sts from front neck holder; pick up and k 30[30,31,31] sts evenly up right side of front neck and down right back neck to complete rnd. 106[106,112,112] sts.
Place a st marker on RH needle to mark beg of rnd and working in rnds (RS always facing), work k1, p1 rib for 15cm (6in).
Cast off loosely and evenly in rib.

SLEEVES
With 3¾mm (US 3) needles, cast on 44[46,48,50] sts.
Work k1, p1 rib for 7cm (2¾in).
Inc row (WS): Keeping continuity of rib, rib 4[0,1,2]; ★m1, rib 4[5,5,5]; rep from ★ to last 4[1,2,3] sts; m1; rib 4[1,2,3]. 54[56,58,60] sts.

Turn book sideways to read chart

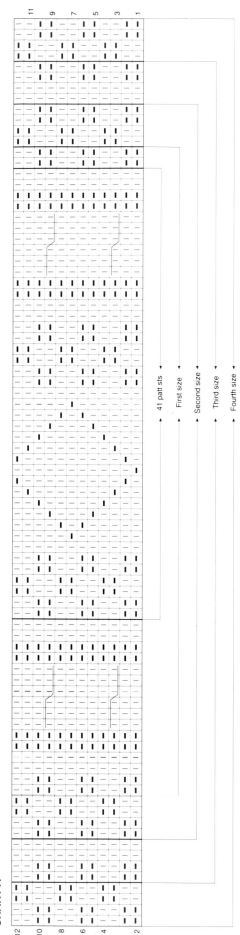

CHART A

CHART B

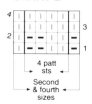

4 patt sts

Second & fourth sizes

KEY

☐ k on RS rows; p on WS rows.

▬ p on RS rows; k on WS rows.

sl first 3 sts to cn and hold at front; k3; k3 from cn.

Change to 3¾mm (US 5) needles and beg with a k row, work in st st, inc 1 st at each end of every foll 4th row until there are 88[90,92,94] sts.

Reading chart B from right to left for RS rows and from left to right for WS rows, set patt as follows—

Chart row 1 (RS): Work first 0[1,0,1] st of row 1 of chart B as indicated; rep 4 patt sts 22[22,23,23] times; work last 0[1,0,1] st of chart as indicated.

Cont in chart B patt as set, work 2 rows more without shaping.

Rep 4 patt rows throughout, inc 1 st at each end of next and every foll 4th row until there are 110[112,116,118] sts, working all increased sts into patt.

Work in chart B patt as set without shaping until sleeve measures 53[54,55, 56]cm (21[21¼,21¾,22]in) from beg. Cast off all sts.

FINISHING

Following instructions on yarn label, wash and dry all knitted pieces, plus approx 5m (6yd) of yarn for sewing up. This will allow the garment pieces to shrink to finished size (see SPECIAL NOTE at beginning of instructions).

Place markers 25[25.5,26.5,27]cm (10[10¼,10½,10¾]in) down from shoulder seam at each side of back and front. Place centre top of sleeve at shoulder seam and sew sleeves to body between markers. Press seams very lightly on WS.

Sew up side and sleeve seams and press seams very lightly on WS, omitting ribs.

*S*houlders on Filey ganseys were often emphasised with a 'rig and furrow' pattern, named after its resemblance to the ridges and furrows of a newly ploughed field. The body pattern – or a simple textured pattern – was worked on the top half of the sleeve, with the lower half worked in stocking stitch. All of the pattern features favoured in Filey are included in this design, but they are given a new twist with an unshrunk indigo dyed cotton yarn. Though not traditional, the yarn reminds me very much of the effect of wind and salt water on well worn ganseys, which became even more beautiful because this type of aging process emphasised the texture of the patterns. Filey is designed to be worked in flat pieces, without gussets. The pieces are shrunk to fit before they are sewn together. Because of the shrinkage in length, the yarn is not suitable for use with the traditional circular style.

Knitted measurements

A = 56.5[59.5,63,66]cm   22$^{1/2}$[23$^{3/4}$,25,26$^{1/2}$]in

B = 77.5[80,82,84]cm   30$^{1/2}$[31$^{1/2}$,32$^{1/4}$,33]in

E = 53[54,55,56]cm   21[21$^{1/4}$,21$^{3/4}$,22]in

Washed Measurements

A = 56.5[59.5,63,66]cm   22$^{1/2}$[23$^{3/4}$,25,26$^{1/2}$]in

B = 65[67.5,69.5,71.5]cm   25$^{1/2}$[26$^{1/2}$,27$^{1/4}$,28]in

C = 40[42,43,44.5]cm   15$^{1/2}$[16$^{1/4}$,16$^{3/4}$,17$^{1/4}$]in

D = 25[25.5,26.5,27]cm   10[10$^{1/4}$,10$^{1/2}$,10$^{0/4}$]in

E = 45[46,47,48]cm   17$^{3/4}$[18,18$^{1/2}$,18$^{3/4}$]in

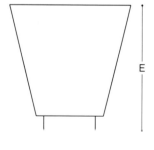
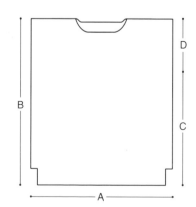

IRELAND

The Irish knitters from Aran knitted ganseys in the
Scottish style until they developed their own
famed Aran sweaters in the 1930's. These were based
on complex cabled forms worked in a heavy yarn.

INISHMORE

SIZES

To fit small [medium, large]
Directions for larger sizes are given in brackets.
Where there is only one set of figures, it applies
to all sizes.

KNITTED MEASUREMENTS

Underarm 114[122,129]cm (45[48,51]in)
Length—
Short version 46[48,51]cm (18¼[19, 20¼]in)
Long version 65[67.5,70]cm (25¾[26¾, 27¾]in)
Sleeve length 46[47,48]cm (18[18½,19]in)

MATERIALS

Yarn weight used: Aran weight pure
wool yarn
Short version: 10[11,11] x 100g (3½oz)
hanks of Rowan *Magpie* in shade no. 608
'Sealord'
Long version: 13[14,15] x 100g (3½oz)
hanks of Rowan *Magpie* in shade no. 002
'Natural'
1 pair each of 3¾mm (US 5) and 4mm
(US 6) needles
1 set of double-pointed *or* short circular
3¾mm (US 5) needles
1 cable needle and 4 stitch holders
Stitch markers

TENSION (GAUGE)

22 sts and 28 rows to 10cm (4in)
measured over Moss st, using 4mm (US 6)
needles

MOSS STITCH

To check tension (gauge) work Moss st
over an odd number of sts as follows—
Row 1 (RS): K1; *p1, k1; rep from * to
end of row.
Rows 2 and 3: P1; *k1, p1; rep from *
to end of row.
Row 4: As row 1.
Rep these 4 rows.

BACK

★★With 3¾mm (US 5) needles, cast on
127[133,139] sts.

*I wanted to develop an Aran-style
design based on the crisp lines of
twisted-stitch patterns set against the
geometry of the diamond shape and
contrasting textures. I have done this
with* Inishmore *by aligning the
centre diamond panel with the
zigzag panels at each side so that
the alternating textures of purl,
moss stitch and twisted rib are
harmoniously contained within the
extended geometry.*

Reading chart A from right to left for RS
(odd-numbered) rows and from left to
right for WS (even-numbered) rows, set
rib patt as follows—
Row 1 (RS): Rep 6 patt sts of row 1 of
chart A 21[22,23] times; work last st of
chart as indicated.
Row 2: Work first st of row 2 of chart A
as indicated; rep 6 patt sts 21[22,23] times.
Cont in patt as set, rep 6 patt rows of
chart A, until rib measures 8cm (3in),
ending with WS facing for next row.

Inc row (WS): Keeping continuity of
rib, rib 9[8,7]; *m1, rib 4; rep from * to
last 10[9,8] sts; m1; rib 10[9,8].
155[163,171] sts.
Change to 4mm (US 6) needles and beg
all charts from row 1, set patt as follows—
Chart row 1 (RS): Work Moss st over
first 9[13,17] sts; work chart B over next
38 sts; work chart C over next 15 sts;
work chart D over next 31 sts; work chart
E over next 15 sts; work chart B over
next 38 sts; work Moss st over last
9[13,17] sts.★★
Cont in patts as set, rep all rows of each
chart until back measures 43[45,48]cm
(17[17¾,19]in) from beg for short version
or 62[64.5,67]cm (24½[25½,26½]in) from
beg for long version, ending with RS
facing for next row.
Next row: Cast off first 54[57,61] sts, but
during cast off — dec 1 st at beg and end
of first chart B cable, dec 3 sts evenly across
centre chart B cable and dec 1 st at beg
and end of third chart B cable; work next
47[49,49] sts in patt, including st already
on needle after cast off and place these
sts on a holder; cast off rem 54[51,61]
sts, dec over chart B cables during cast off
as before.

FRONT

Work as back from ★★ to ★★.
Cont in patts as set, rep all rows of each
chart until front measures 14[16,16] rows
fewer than back to shoulder, ending with
RS facing for next row.
Shape Front Neck
Next row (RS): Keeping continuity,
work 62[66,70] sts in patt; place next 31
sts on a holder; turn, leaving rem sts on a
spare needle.
Keeping continuity of patt as far as
possible throughout, shape left side of
neck as follows—
★★★Dec 1 st at neck edge on every foll
row 4 times, then at same edge on every
foll alt row 4[5,5] times.
54[57,61] sts rem.
Work 1 row without shaping, ending
with RS facing for next row.
Cast off shoulder sts, dec over chart B
cables during cast off as for back.★★★

CHART C

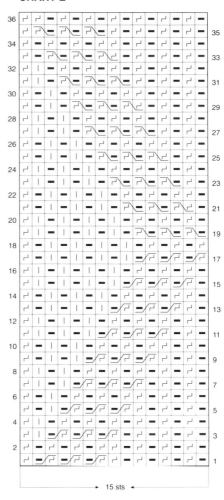

← 15 sts →

KEY

| ⊥ | k on RS rows; p on WS rows. |

| ▬ | p on RS rows; k on WS rows. |

| ⅃ | k into back of st on RS rows; p into back of st on WS rows. |

sl first 2 sts to cn and hold at front; k into back of next st; sl the p st from cn back onto left needle and p it; k into back of rem st on cn.

sl first st to cn and hold at back; k into back of next st; p1 from cn.

sl first st to cn and hold at front; p1; k into back of st from cn.

sl first 2 sts to cn and hold at back; k2; k2 from cn.

sl first 2 sts to cn and hold at front; k2; k2 from cn.

sl first 3 sts to cn and hold at front; k1b, p1, k1b, p1; k1b, p1, k1b from cn.

sl first 4 sts to cn and hold at back; k1b, p1, k1b; p1, k1b, p1, k1b from cn.

CHART E

← 15 sts →

CHART B

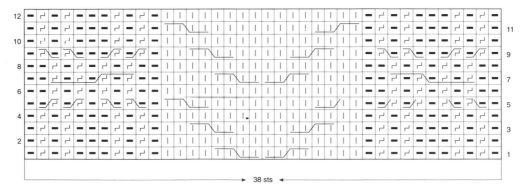

← 38 sts →

CHART F

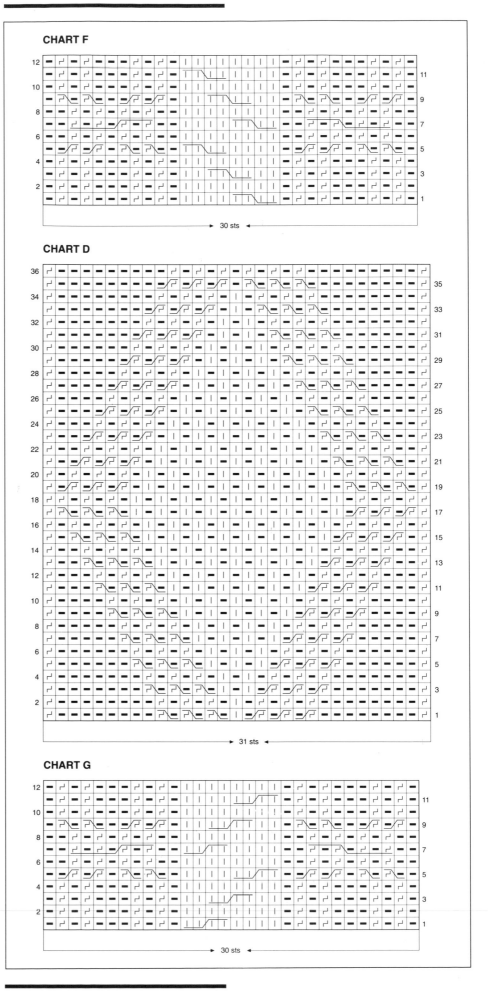

With RS facing, rejoin yarn to sts of right side of neck, and keeping continuity, work 1 row in patt without shaping, then complete as left side of neck from ★★★ to ★★★.

CHART A

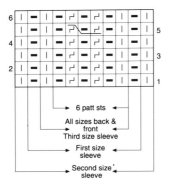

→ 6 patt sts ←
All sizes back & → front
Third size sleeve
→ First size sleeve
→ Second size sleeve

LEFT SLEEVE

★★With 3¾mm (US 5) needles, cast on 51[53,55] sts.

Beg chart A from row 1, set rib patt as follows—

Row 1 (RS): Work first 1[2,0] sts of row 1 of chart A as indicated; rep 6 patt sts 8[8,9] times; work last 2[3,1] sts of chart as indicated.

Row 2: Work first 2[3,1] sts of row 2 of chart A as indicated; rep 6 patt sts 8[8,9] times; work last 1[2,0] sts of chart as indicated.

Cont in patt as set, rep 6 patt rows of chart A, until cuff measures 7cm (2¾in), ending with WS facing for next row.

Inc row (WS): Keeping continuity of rib, rib 2[3,4]; *m1, rib 2; rep from * to last 3[4,5] sts; m1; rib 3[4,5]. 75[77,79] sts.★★

Change to 4mm (US 6) needles and beg all charts from row 1, set patt as follows—

Chart row 1 (RS): Work Moss st over first 0[1,2] sts; work chart F over next 30 sts; work chart C over next 15 sts; work chart G over next 30 sts; work Moss st over last 0[1,2] sts.

★★★Cont in patts as set, rep all rows of each chart and inc 1 st at each end of 3rd and every foll 4th row until there are 125[129,131] sts, working all increased sts in Moss st.

Work in patt without shaping until sleeve

CHART D

CHART G

A bold design, Inishmore is effective in the traditional natural colour and standard length or in a dark shade and cropped style. Further choice is yours with either a crew neckband or a cosy roll collar. In the standard length, Inishmore looks equally good on a man (see page 69) or a woman, as do most fisher ganseys.

measures 46[47,48]cm (18[18½,19]in) from beg, ending with RS facing for next row.

Shape Saddle
Keeping continuity, cast off 54[56,57] sts at beg of next 2 rows, dec 1 st at beg and end of all 3 chart F cables and all 3 chart G cables during cast offs. 17 sts.
Work these sts in patt as set, until saddle fits in length along shoulder cast-off edge. Place sts on a holder.

RIGHT SLEEVE
Work as left sleeve from ** to **.
Change to 4mm (US 6) needles and beg all charts from row 1, set patt as follows—
Chart row 1 (RS): Work Moss st over first 0[1,2] sts; work chart F over next 30 sts; work chart E over next 15 sts; work chart G over next 30 sts; work Moss st over last 0[1,2] sts.
Complete as for left sleeve from ***.

FINISHING
Do not press pieces.
Place markers 21[22,22.5]cm (8¼[8½, 8¾]in) down from shoulder cast off at each side of back and front. Pin saddles along back and front shoulder cast-off edges and sew in place. Place each end of top of sleeve at markers on front and back, and sew sleeves to body.
Press seams very lightly on WS.
Sew up side and sleeve seams and press seams very lightly on WS, omitting ribs.

CREW NECKBAND
With RS facing and double-pointed needles or circular 3¾mm (US 5) needle, beg at back neck st holder and pick up sts as follows—
From back neck holder — k2[3,3]; (k2tog, k5) 6 times; k2tog; k1[2,2]; there are now 40[42,42] sts on needle; from left saddle holder — *(k2tog, k3) 3 times; k2tog*; there are now 53[55,55] sts on needle; pick up and k 11[13,13] sts evenly down left side of front neck to front neck holder; from front neck holder — k1; (k2tog, k5) 4 times; k2tog; there are now 90[94,94] sts on needle; pick up and k 11[13,13] sts evenly up right front neck; from right saddle holder work as from * to * to complete rnd. 114[120,120] sts.
Place a st marker on RH needle to mark beg of rnd, then working in rnds (RS always facing) and beg chart A from rnd 1 (reading all chart rnds from right to left), rep 6 patt sts 19[20,20] times in each rnd and rep 6 patt rnds until neckband measures 6cm (2½in).
Cast off loosely and evenly in rib.

ROLL COLLAR
Turn garment wrong side out and pick up and dec sts as for crew neckband, but purl all sts during the process.
Keep wrong side out and work patt as for crew neckband until collar measures 15cm (6in).
Cast off evenly in rib.

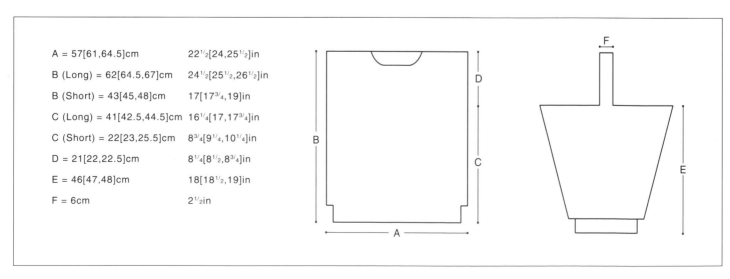

A = 57[61,64.5]cm   22½[24,25½]in

B (Long) = 62[64.5,67]cm   24½[25½,26½]in

B (Short) = 43[45,48]cm   17[17¾,19]in

C (Long) = 41[42.5,44.5]cm   16¼[17,17¾]in

C (Short) = 22[23,25.5]cm   8¾[9¼,10¼]in

D = 21[22,22.5]cm   8¼[8½,8¾]in

E = 46[47,48]cm   18[18½,19]in

F = 6cm   2½in

INISHMAAN

RATING ★ ★

SIZES
To fit small [medium, large]
*Directions for larger sizes are given in brackets.
Where there is only one set of figures, it applies
to all sizes.*

KNITTED
MEASUREMENTS
Underarm 114[122,131]cm (45[48,52]in)
Length 67.5[70,72.5]cm (26½[27½,28½]in)
Sleeve length 46[47,48]cm (18[18½,19]in)

MATERIALS
Yarn weight used: Aran weight pure
wool yarn
12[13,14] x 100g (3½oz) hanks of Rowan
Magpie in shade no. 612 'Neptune'
1 pair each of 4mm (US 6) and 5mm
(US 8) needles
1 set of double-pointed *or* short circular
3¾mm (US 5) needles
1 cable needle
4 stitch holders
Stitch markers

TENSION (GAUGE)
19 sts and 24 rows to 10cm (4in)
measured over sand st, using 5mm (US 8)
needles

SAND STITCH
To check tension (gauge) work sand st
over an odd number of sts as follows—
Row 1 (RS): *K1, p1; rep from * to last
st; k1.
Row 2: Knit.
Rep these 2 rows.

FRONT
**With 4mm (US 6) needles, cast on
122[130,138] sts.
Reading chart A (page 64) from right to
left for RS (odd-numbered) rows and
from left to right for WS (even-numbered)
rows, set rib and cable patt as follows—
Row 1 (RS): (P2, k2) 2[3,4] times; work
row 1 of chart A over next 8 sts; *k2;
work chart A over next 8 sts; (k2, p2, k2,
work chart A over next 8 sts) twice*; (k2,
p2) 3 times; rep from * to * once; k2;

*F*or Inishmaan, *the theme in my
mind's eye was a play on narrow
vertical columns of soft curving cables
and interlaced lines. I have added a
touch of intricacy by placing different
interlaced panels at the centre front
and back. Textural contrast comes in
the form of narrow laddered knot
panels. The long slim look is
emphasised by running the chain
cables through the ribs.*

work chart A over next 8 sts; (k2, p2)
2[3,4] times.
Row 2: K the k sts and p the p sts as they
appear and work row 2 of chart A over
cabled sts.
Cont in patt as set, rep 4 patt rows of
chart A, and work 23 rows in total,
ending with WS facing for next row.
Inc row (WS): Keeping continuity of
rib, rib 1[3,4]; (m1, rib 3[3,4]) twice; m1;
rib 1[3,4]; work row 4 of chart A over
next 8 sts; m1; rib 2; m1; work chart A

over next 8 sts; rib 3; m1; rib 3; *work
chart A over next 8 sts; (rib 2, m1)
twice; rib 2; work chart A over next 8
sts*; rib 1; m1; rib 3; m1; (rib 2, m1) 3
times; rib 3; m1; rib 1; rep from * to *
once; rib 3; m1; rib 3; work chart A over
next 8 sts; m1; rib 2; m1; work chart A
over next 8 sts; rib 1[3,4]; (m1, rib 3[3,4])
twice; m1; rib 1[3,4]. 144[152,160] sts.
Change to 5mm (US 8) needles and beg
all charts from row 1, set patt as follows—
Chart row 1 (RS): Work sand st over
first 11[15,19] sts; work chart A over next
8 sts; work chart B over next 4 sts; work
chart A over next 8 sts; work chart C over
next 7 sts; work chart A over next 8 sts;
work chart D over next 8 sts; work chart
A over next 8 sts; work chart E over next
20 sts; work chart A over next 8 sts; work
chart D over next 8 sts; work chart A over
next 8 sts; work chart C over next 7 sts;
work chart A over next 8 sts; work chart F
over next 4 sts; work chart A over next 8
sts; work sand st over last 11[15,19] sts.★★★
Cont in patts as set, rep all rows of each
chart until front measures 57.5[60,62.5]cm
(22½[23½,24½]in), ending with RS facing
for next row.

Shape Front Neck
Next row (RS): Keeping continuity,
work 62[66,70] sts in patt; place next 20
sts on a holder; turn, leaving rem sts on a
spare needle.
Keeping continuity of patt as far as
possible throughout, shape left side of
neck as follows—
****Cast off 3 sts at beg of next row and
foll alt row. 56[60,64] sts.
Work 1 row without shaping. Cast off 2
sts at beg of next row. 54[58,62] sts.
Dec 1 st at neck edge on every foll row 6
times. Work 1 row without shaping.
Dec 1 st at neck edge on next row.
47[51,55] sts rem.
Cast off rem sts, dec 1 st at centre of chart
A and chart B cables during cast off.*****
With RS facing, rejoin yarn to sts of right
side of neck, and keeping continuity,
work 2 rows in patt without shaping, then
complete as left side of neck from **** to
*****, dec 1 st at centre of chart A and
chart F cables during cast off.

An interesting and fun design to knit, Inishmaan will look wonderful worked in your favourite colour. The interlaced panel at the centre back (left) is different from the centre front panel.

Cont in patt as set, inc 1 st at each end of every foll 4th row until there are 106[110,112] sts in total, working these increased sts in sand st throughout. Work in patt without shaping until sleeve measures 46[47,48]cm (18[18½,19]in) from beg, ending with RS facing for next row.

Shape Saddle
Keeping continuity, cast off 41[43,44] sts at beg of next 2 rows, dec 1 st at centre of charts A, B and F cables during cast offs. Cont working charts A and D as set without shaping over rem 24 sts of sleeve until saddle fits in length along shoulder cast-off edge.
Place sts on a holder.

FINISHING

Do not press pieces.
Place markers 21[22,22.5]cm (8¼[8½,8¾]in) down from shoulder cast off at each side of back and front. Sew saddles along shoulder cast-off edges of back and front. Place each end of top of sleeve at markers on front and back, and sew sleeves to body.
Press seams very lightly on WS.
Sew up side and sleeve seams and press seams very lightly on WS, omitting ribs.

NECKBAND

With RS facing and double-pointed needles or circular 3¾mm (US 5) needle, beg at back neck st holder and pick up sts as follows—
From back neck holder — k2; k2tog; k3; p2; k4; p2; k2tog; k2; (k2tog; k1; k2tog; k2) twice; k2tog; p2; k4; p2; k3; k2tog; k2; there are now 42 sts on needle; from left saddle holder — *p2; k4; p2; k1; k2tog; k2; k2tog; k1; p2; k4; p2*; there are now 64 sts on needle; pick up and k 17 sts evenly down left side of front neck

BACK

Work as front from ** to ***, but working chart G instead of chart E over 20 centre sts of back.
Cont in patt as set, rep all rows of charts until there are same number of chart rows as front to shoulder cast off, ending with RS facing for next row.

Shape Shoulders
Next row (RS): Cast off first 47[51,55] sts, dec 1 st at centre of chart A and chart B cables during cast off; keeping continuity, work next 50 sts in patt and place these sts on a holder; work rem 47[51,55] sts in patt.
Cast off rem sts, dec 1 st at centre of chart A and chart F cables during cast off.

SLEEVES

With 4mm (US 6) needles, cast on 50[52,54] sts.
Beg chart A from row 1, set rib and cable patt as follows—
Row 1 (RS): P0[1,2]; (k2, p2) 3 times; k2; work row 1 of chart A over next 8 sts; k2; p2; k2; work chart A over next 8 sts; (k2, p2) 3 times; k2; p0[1,2].

Row 2: K the k sts and p the p sts as they appear and work row 2 of chart A over cabled sts.
Cont in patt as set, rep 4 patt rows of chart A, and work 19 rows in total, ending with WS facing for next row.
Inc row (WS): Keeping continuity of rib, rib 2[1,2]; (m1, rib 3) 4 times; m1; rib 0[2,2]; work row 4 of chart A over next 8 sts; (rib 2, m1) twice; rib 2; work chart A over next 8 sts; rib 0[2,2]; (m1, rib 3) 4 times; m1; rib 2[1,2]. 62[64,66] sts.
Change to 5mm (US 8) needles and beg all charts from row 1, set patt as follows—
Chart row 1 (RS): P0[1,2]; work chart B over next 4 sts; work chart A over next 8 sts; work chart C over next 7 sts; work chart A over next 8 sts; work chart D over next 8 sts; work chart A over next 8 sts; work chart C over next 7 sts; work chart A over next 8 sts; work chart F over next 4 sts; p0[1,2].
Cont in patts as set, rep all rows of each chart and inc 1 st at each end of 2nd and foll 3rd row, working 2 sts before chart B and 2 sts after chart F in rev st st and all rem edge sts in sand st.

KEY

| k on RS rows; p on WS rows.

− p on RS rows; k on WS rows.

sl first st to cn and hold at back; k1; k1 from cn.

sl first st to cn and hold at front; k1; k1 from cn.

sl first 2 sts to cn and hold at back; k2; k2 from cn.

sl first 2 sts to cn and hold at front; k2; k2 from cn.

K make knot thus – (k1, p1) twice into same st, then sl the first 3 sts made over the last st made.

sl first 2 sts to cn and hold at back; k2; p2 from cn.

sl first 2 sts to cn and hold at front; p2; k2 from cn.

sl first 3 sts to cn and hold at back; k3; k3 from cn.

sl first 3 sts to cn and hold at front; k3; k3 from cn.

sl first st to cn and hold at back; k3; p1 from cn.

sl first 3 sts to cn and hold at front; p1; k3 from cn.

CHART A

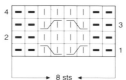

◄ 8 sts ◄

CHART B

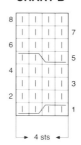

◄ 4 sts ◄

CHART D

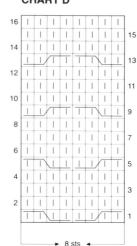

◄ 8 sts ◄

CHART C

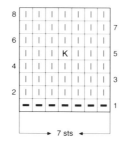

◄ 7 sts ◄

CHART F

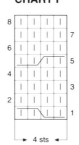

◄ 4 sts ◄

CHART E

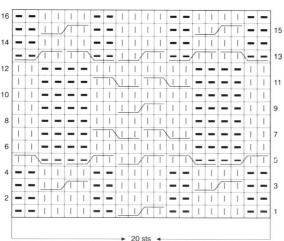

◄ 20 sts ◄

CHART G

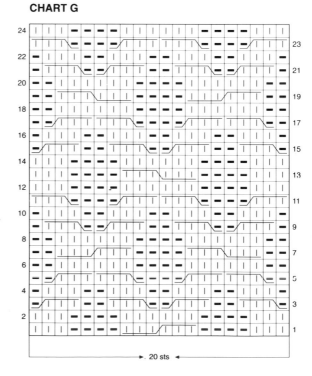

◄ 20 sts ◄

to front neck holder; from front neck holder — k3; k2tog; (k2, k2tog) 3 times; k3; pick up and k 17 sts evenly up right front neck; from right saddle holder work as from ★ to ★ to complete rnd. 136 sts. Place a st marker on RH needle to mark beg of rnd, then working in rnds (RS always facing) and beg chart A from row 1 (reading all chart rnds from right to left), set rib and cable patt as follows—

Rnd 1: K2; p2; k2; ★work chart A over next 8 sts; (k2, p2) 3 times; k2; work chart A over next 8 sts★; (k2; p2; k2; work chart A over next 8 sts) twice; (k2, p2) twice; k2; rep from ★ to ★ once; (k2, p2) twice; k2; work chart A over next 8 sts; k2; p2; k2; work chart A over last 8 sts. Cont in patt as set, rep 4 patt rnds of chart A as set, until neckband measures 7cm (2¾in).

Cast off all k sts knitwise and all p sts purlwise, dec 1 st at centre of each chart A cable during cast off.

Darn in loose ends.

*T*he beautiful sculpted forms of traditional Aran patterns have always held a particular fascination for me, and I love to experiment with the different elements in this style.

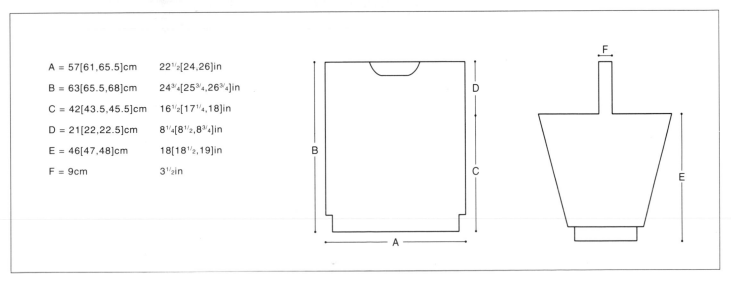

A = 57[61,65.5]cm   22½[24,26]in

B = 63[65.5,68]cm   24¾[25¾,26¾]in

C = 42[43.5,45.5]cm   16½[17¼,18]in

D = 21[22,22.5]cm   8¼[8½,8¾]in

E = 46[47,48]cm   18[18½,19]in

F = 9cm   3½in

INISHEER

SIZES
To fit age 4-5[6-7,8-9] or 58-61[63-66, 68-71]cm (23-24[25-26,27-28]in) chest
Directions for larger sizes are given in brackets. Where there is only one set of figures, it applies to all sizes.

KNITTED MEASUREMENTS
Underarm 76[82,92]cm (30[32½,36]in)
Length 39[42,45]cm (15½[16½,18]in)
Sleeve length 29[31.5,34]cm (11½[12½, 13½]in)

MATERIALS
Yarn weight used: double knitting wool (US knitting worsted)
8[9,11] x 50g (1¾oz) balls of Rowan *Designer DK* in shade no. 649 Off-white
1 pair each of 3¼mm (US 3) and 3¾mm (US 5) needles
1 set of double-pointed 3¼mm (US 3) needles
1 cable needle
2 stitch holders
Stitch markers

TENSION (GAUGE)
26 sts and 34 rows to 10cm (4in) measured over sand st, using 3¾mm (US 5) needles

SAND STITCH
To check tension (gauge) work sand st over an even number of sts as follows—
Row 1 (RS): *K1, p1; rep from * to end of row.
Row 2: Knit.
Rep these 2 rows.

BACK
**With 3¼mm (US 3) needles, cast on 102[107,117] sts.
Reading chart A from right to left for RS (odd numbered) rows and from left to right for WS (even-numbered) rows, set rib patt as follows—
Row 1 (RS): Rep 5 patt sts of row 1 of chart A 20[21,23] times; work last 2 sts of chart as indicated.

*A*lthough traditional Aran sweaters are synonymous with heavy sculpted forms, openwork patterns were occasionally used. I have used this idea to create a light and delicate Aran design for a child in sizes for ages four to nine years. The curves, textures and openwork of the centre panels on Inisheer are complemented by the light cables and the twisted-stitch patterns.

Row 2: Work first 2 sts of row 2 of chart A as indicated; rep 5 patt sts 20[21,23] times.
Cont in patt as set, rep 8 patt rows of chart A until rib measures 5[5,6]cm (2[2,2½]in), ending with WS facing for next row.
Inc row (WS): P2[2,1]; *m1, p7[6,6]; rep from * to last 2[3,2] sts; m1; p2[3,2]. 117[125,137] sts.
Change to 3¾mm (US 5) needles and beg all charts from row 1, set patt as follows—
Chart row 1 (RS): Work sand st over first 10[14,20] sts; work chart B over next 9 sts; work chart C over next 11 sts; work chart D over next 9 sts; work chart E over next 13 sts; work chart F over next 13 sts; work chart E over next 13 sts; work chart G over next 9 sts; work chart H over next 11 sts; work chart B over next 9 sts; work sand st over last 10[14,20] sts.**
Cont in patts as set, rep all rows of each chart until back measures 38[41,44]cm (15[16,17½]in) from beg, ending with RS facing for next row.
Shape Back Neck
Next row: Keeping continuity, work 38[41,46] sts in patt; place next 41[43,45] sts on a holder; turn, leaving rem st on a spare needle.
Keeping continuity of patt as far as possible throughout, shape right side of neck as follows—
***Cast off 3 sts at beg of next row.
Work 1 row without shaping.
Cast off 2 sts at beg of next row.
Cast off rem 33[36,41] sts.***
With RS facing, rejoin yarn to sts of left side of neck, and keeping continuity, work 2 rows without shaping, then complete as right neck from *** to ***.

FRONT
Work as back from ** to **.
Cont in patts as set, rep all rows of each chart until front measures 33.5[36, 38.5]cm (13¼[14,15¼]in) from beg, ending with RS facing for next row.
Shape Front Neck
Next row (RS): Keeping continuity, work 48[51,56] sts in patt; place next 21[23,25] sts on a holder; turn, leaving rem sts on a spare needle.
Keeping continuity of patt as far as possible throughout, shape left side of neck as follows—
***Cast off 4[3,3] sts at beg of next row.
Work 1 row without shaping.
Cast off 3[3,2] sts at beg of next row.
Dec 1 st at neck edge on every foll row 8 times, then at same edge on every foll alt row 0[1,2] times. 33[36,41] sts rem.
Work without shaping until there are same number of rows as back to shoulder, ending at armhole edge.

CHART A

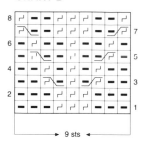

→ 5 patt sts ←

→ Last 2 sts

CHART B

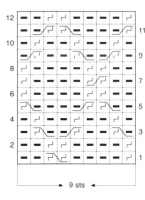

→ 9 sts ←

CHART C

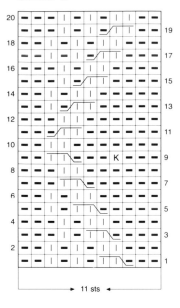

→ 11 sts ←

CHART D

→ 9 sts ←

CHART E

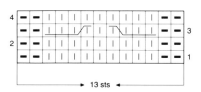

→ 13 sts ←

CHART H

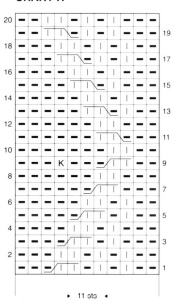

→ 11 sts ←

KEY

│ k on RS rows; p on WS rows.

─ p on RS rows; k on WS rows.

ↄ k into back of st on RS rows; p into back of st on WS rows.

sl first st to cn and hold at front; p1; k into back of st from cn.

sl first st to cn and hold at back; k into back of next st; p1 from cn.

sl first 2 sts to cn and hold at front; p1; k2 from cn.

sl first st to cn and hold at back; k2; p1 from cn.

K make knot thus – (k1, p1) twice into same st, then sl the first 3 sts made over the last st made.

sl first st to cn and hold at front; k3; k1 from cn.

sl first 3 sts to cn and hold at back; k1; k3 from cn.

sl first st to cn and hold at front; k1b; k1b from cn.

sl first st to cn and hold at back; k1b; k1b from cn.

◿ p2tog.

◬ p3tog.

○ yo.

CHART F

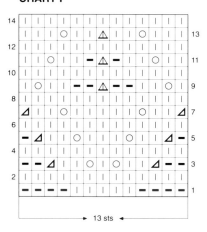

→ 13 sts ←

CHART G

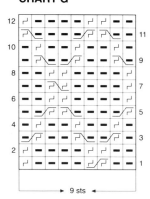

→ 9 sts ←

CHART I

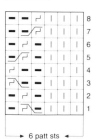

→ 6 patt sts ←

The use of a lighter double knitting wool has reduced the scale of the patterns on Inisheer *and emphasised the detail. (Instructions for* Inishmore, *the man's gansey pictured left, are given on page 57.)*

Cast off all sts.★★★
With RS facing, rejoin yarn to sts of right side of neck, and keeping continuity, work 2 rows in patt without shaping, then complete as left side of neck from ★★★ to ★★★.

SLEEVES

With 3¼mm (US 3) needles, cast on 45[47,52] sts.
Beg chart A from row 1, set rib patt as follows—
Row 1 (RS): Rep 5 patt sts of row 1 of chart A 9[9,10] times; work last 0[2,2] sts of chart.
Row 2: Work first 0[2,2] sts of row 2 of chart A; rep 5 patt sts 9[9,10] times.
Cont in patt as set, rep 8 patt rows of chart A until cuff measures 4[5,5]cm (1½[2,2]in), ending with WS facing for next row.
Inc row (WS): P4[1,1]; ★m1, p4[4,5]; rep from ★ to last 5[2,1] sts; m1; p5[2,1]. 55[59,63] sts.
Change to 3¼mm (US 5) needles and beg

all charts from row 1, set patt as follows—
Chart row 1 (RS): Work sand st over first 8[10,12] sts; work chart E over next 13 sts; work chart F over next 13 sts; work chart E over next 13 sts; work sand st over last 8[10,12] sts.
Cont in patts as set, rep all rows of each chart and inc 1 st at each end of every foll 3rd row until there are 77[89,93] sts, then on every foll 4th row until there are 99[109,117] sts, working all increased sts in sand st.
Work in patt without shaping until sleeve measures 29[31.5,34]cm (11½[12½,13½]in). Cast off all sts.

FINISHING

Do not press pieces.
Place markers 17.5[19.5,21]cm (7[7¾, 8¼]in) down from shoulder cast off at each side of back and front. Sew back and front tog at shoulder seams. Place centre top of sleeves at shoulder seams and sew sleeves to body between markers.
Press seams very lightly on WS.

Sew up side and sleeve seams and press seams very lightly on WS, omitting ribs.

NECKBAND

With RS facing and double-pointed 3¼mm (US 3) needles, beg at back neck st holder and pick up sts as follows—
(K4[5,6]; k2tog; k1; k2tog; k23; k2tog; k1; k2tog; k4[5,6]) all from back neck holder; there are now 37[39,41] sts on needle; pick up and k 22[23,24] sts evenly up left back neck and down left side of front neck to front neck holder; k 21[23,25] sts from front neck holder; pick up and k 22[23,24] sts evenly up right front neck and down right back neck to complete rnd. 102[108,114] sts.
Place a st marker on RH needle to mark beg of rnd, then working in rnds (RS always facing) and beg chart I from rnd 1 (reading all chart rnds from right to left), rep 6 patt sts 17[18,19] times in each rnd and rep 8 patt rnds until neckband measures 4[5,5]cm (1½[2,2]in).
Cast off loosely and evenly knitwise.

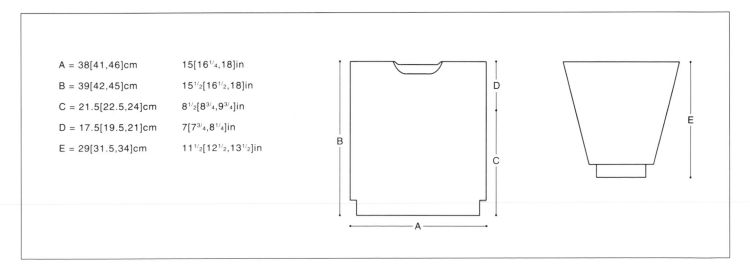

A = 38[41,46]cm   15[16¼,18]in

B = 39[42,45]cm   15½[16½,18]in

C = 21.5[22.5,24]cm   8½[8¾,9¾]in

D = 17.5[19.5,21]cm   7[7¾,8¼]in

E = 29[31.5,34]cm   11½[12½,13½]in

KINSALE

RATING ★★

SIZES

To fit small [medium, large]
*Directions for larger sizes are given in brackets.
Where there is only one set of figures, it applies
to all sizes.*

KNITTED MEASUREMENTS

Underarm 106[115,126]cm (42½[46, 50½]in)
Length 66[69,71]cm (26[27¼,28]in)
Sleeve length 44.5[46,48] (17½[18,19]in)

MATERIALS

Yarn weight used: 4-ply wool and cotton (US sport)
13[14,15] x 50g (1½oz) balls of *Rowan Wool and Cotton* in shade no. 927 'Mandala'
1 pair of 3mm (US 3) needles
1 set of 4 double-pointed *or* short circular 2¾mm (US 1) needles
2 stitch holders and stitch markers

TENSION (GAUGE)

15 sts and 19 rows to 5cm (2in) measured over chart patt, using 3mm (US 3) needles

BACK

With 3mm (US 3) needles, cast on 144[156,170] sts.
Work border as follows—
Row 1 (RS): Purl.
Row 2: Knit.
Row 3: Knit.
Row 4: Purl.
Rep these 4 rows twice more, then work rows 1-3 once more, thus working 15 rows in total.
Inc row (WS): P2[6,4]; *m1, p10[9,9]; rep from * to last 2[6,4] sts; m1; p2[6,4]. 159[173,189] sts.
Reading chart A from right to left for RS (odd-numbered) rows and from left to right for WS (even-numbered) rows, set patt as follows—
Chart row 1 (RS): Work first 0[7,0] sts of row 1 of chart A as indicated; rep 30 patt sts 5[5,6] times; work last 9[16,9] sts of chart as indicated.

*T*he town of Kinsale in County Cork in Ireland is well known for its plain fishermen's smocks made from heavy cotton fabric. I have used the smock shape, worked in flat pieces, as the backdrop for this graphic knit and purl combination. The play of strong verticals with horizontal and waving lines combines with textured diamonds to produce a design that could be a subtle refrain of the famed Aran style.

Chart row 2: Work first 9[16,9] sts of row 2 of chart A as indicated; rep 30 patt sts 5[5,6] times; work last 0[7,0] sts of chart as indicated.
Cont in chart patt as set, rep 16 patt rows until back measures 65[68,70]cm (25½[26¾,27½]in) from beg, ending with RS facing for next row.
Shape Back Neck
Next row (RS): Keeping continuity, work 56[62,68] sts in patt; place next 47[49,53] sts on a holder; turn, leaving rem sts on a spare needle.
Keeping continuity of patt throughout, shape right side of neck as follows—
★★Cast off 3 sts at beg of next row. 53[59,65] sts.
Work 1 row without shaping.
Cast off 2 sts at beg of next row.
Work 1 row without shaping.
Place rem 51[57,63] sts on a spare needle.★★★
With RS facing, rejoin yarn to sts of left side of neck, and keeping continuity, work 2 rows in patt without shaping, then shape as right side of neck from ★★ to ★★★.

FRONT

Work as back until front measures 59[61.5,63]cm (23¼[24¼,24¾]in) from beg, ending with RS facing for next row.
Shape Front Neck
Next row (RS): Keeping continuity, work 69[75,82] sts in patt; place next 21[23,25] sts on a holder; turn, leaving rem sts on a spare needle.
Keeping continuity of patt throughout, shape left side of neck as follows—
★★Cast off 3 sts at beg of next row. 66[72,79] sts.
Work 1 row without shaping.
Cast off 2 sts at beg of next row. 64[70,77] sts.
Dec 1 st at neck edge on every foll row 6 times, then at same edge of every foll alt row 7[7,8] times. 51[57,63] sts rem.
Work without shaping until there are same number of chart rows as back to shoulder, ending at neck edge.
Place sts on a spare needle.★★★
With RS facing, rejoin yarn to sts of right side of neck, and keeping continuity, work 2 rows in patt without shaping, then shape as left side of front neck from ★★ to ★★★.

NECKBAND

Before beg neckband, join back and front at shoulders as follows—
With 3mm (US 3) needle, holding WS of back and front tog and with RS of back facing, cast off shoulder sts tog in patt.

CHART A

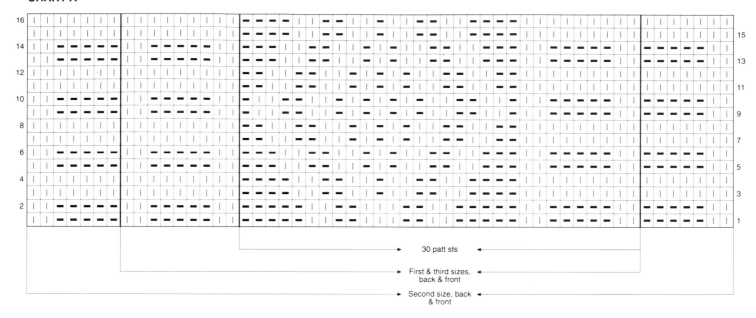

30 patt sts

First & third sizes,
back & front

Second size, back
& front

CHART B

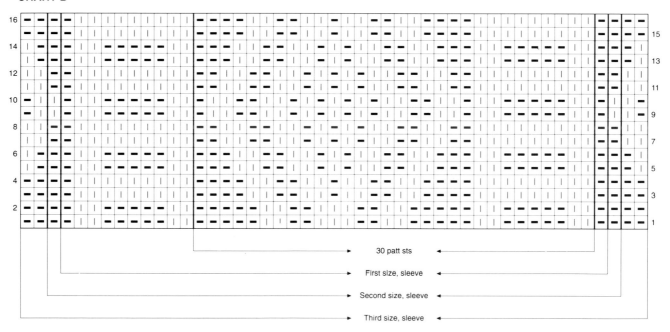

30 patt sts

First size, sleeve

Second size, sleeve

Third size, sleeve

KEY

☐ k on RS rows; p on WS rows.

▬ p on RS rows; k on WS rows.

Begin Neckband

With RS facing and double-pointed or circular 2¾mm (US 1) needles, beg at back neck st holder and pick up sts as follows—

(K2; k2tog; k19[20,22]; k2tog;

k18[19,21]; k2tog; k2) all from back neck holder; pick up and k 28[29,30] sts evenly down left side of front neck to front neck holder; k 21[23,25] sts from front neck holder, dec 1 st at centre front; pick up and k 28[29,30] sts evenly up right side of front neck to complete rnd. 120[126,134] sts. Place a st marker on RH needle to mark beg of rnd and working in rnds (RS always facing), work as follows—

Rnds 1 and 2: Knit.
Rnds 3 and 4: Purl.
Rep these 4 rnds 4 times more, working 20 rnds in total.
Cast off loosely and evenly knitwise.

S L E E V E S

With 3mm (US 3) needles, cast on 62[64,68] sts.
Work 15 rows of border as back.

Inc row (WS): P3[4,2]; *m1, p7[7,8]; rep from * to last 3[4,2] sts; m1; p3[4,2]. 71[73,77] sts.

Reading chart B from right to left for RS rows and from left to right for WS rows, set patt as follows—

Chart row 1 (RS): Work first 1[2,4] sts of row 1 of chart B as indicated; rep 30 patt sts twice; work last 10[11,13] sts of chart as indicated.

Chart row 2: Work first 10[11,13] sts of row 2 of chart B as indicated; rep 30 patt sts twice; work last 1[2,4] sts of chart as indicated.

Cont in chart patt as set, rep 16 patt rows and inc 1 st at each end of 3rd and every foll 4th row until there are 145[149,153] sts, working all increased sts into chart B patt as set.

Work in patt without shaping until sleeve measures 44.5[46,48]cm (17½[18,19]in) from beg.

Cast off all sts.

FINISHING

Do not press pieces.

Place markers 24[25,25.5]cm (9½[10, 10¼]in) down from shoulder seam at each side of back and front.

Place centre top of sleeve at shoulder seam and sew sleeves to body between markers.

Press seams lightly on WS.

Sew up side and sleeve seams and press seams lightly on WS, omitting borders.

The knit and purl ridge pattern on hemline, neckband and cuffs of Kinsale *provides the perfect foil for this fluent and harmonious pattern, knitted here in a soft shade of wool and cotton. This is another design that would also look beautiful worked in 5-ply gansey wool.*

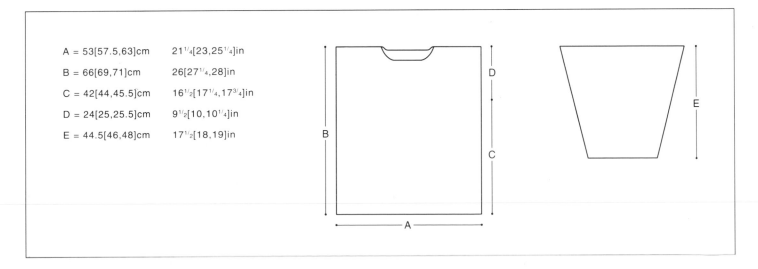

A = 53[57.5,63]cm   21¼[23,25¼]in

B = 66[69,71]cm   26[27¼,28]in

C = 42[44,45.5]cm   16½[17¼,17¾]in

D = 24[25,25.5]cm   9½[10,10¼]in

E = 44.5[46,48]cm   17½[18,19]in

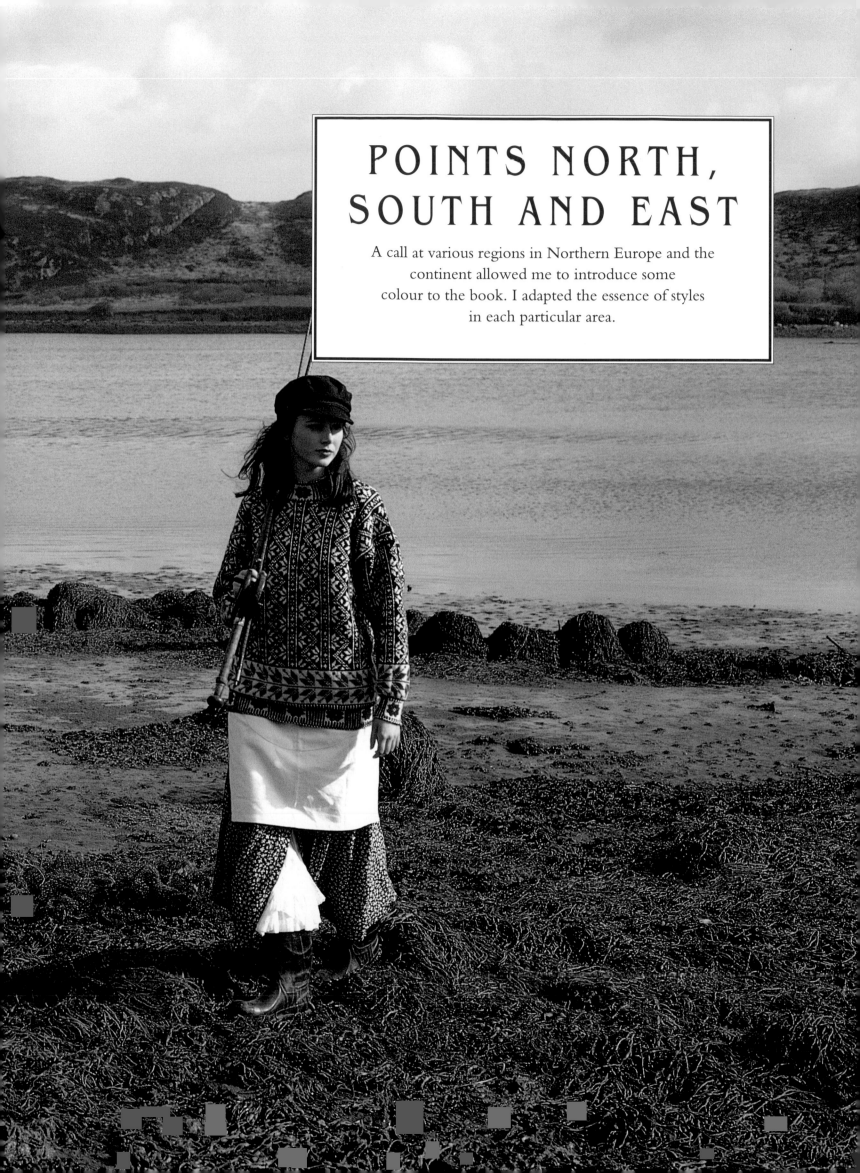

POINTS NORTH,
SOUTH AND EAST

A call at various regions in Northern Europe and the
continent allowed me to introduce some
colour to the book. I adapted the essence of styles
in each particular area.

NORWAY

RATING ★★

SIZE
One size fits all

KNITTED MEASUREMENTS
Underarm, excluding gussets 120cm (48in)
Length 68.5cm (27¼in)
Sleeve length 48cm (19in)

MATERIALS
Yarn weight used: double knitting wool
(US knitting worsted)
9 x 50g (1¾oz) balls of Rowan *Designer DK* in A (shade no. 671 Navy)
8 x 50g (1¾oz) balls of Rowan *Designer DK* in B (shade no. 649 Off-white)
2 x 50g (1¾oz) balls of Rowan *Designer DK* in C (shade no. 673 Red)
1 set of double-pointed *or* circular 3¼mm (US 3) and 3¾mm (US 5) needles
4 stitch holders
Stitch markers

TENSION (GAUGE)
25 sts and 28 rows to 10cm (4in) measured over chart C patt worked in the round (see SPECIAL NOTE), using 3¾mm (US 5) needles

SPECIAL NOTE
All charts are worked in st st.
When working a tension (gauge) swatch in chart C patt, work every row on the RS only, breaking off yarns at the end of every row. (See page 123 for making a Fair Isle swatch.)

BODY
Body is worked in one piece to armhole, then steeks are added at armhole and body is cont in the rnd to shoulders.
With 3¼mm (US 3) needles and using yarns A and B alternately, cast on 280 sts. (See pages 118 and 119 for working a two colour cast on.)
Place a st marker on RH needle to mark beg of rnd, then making sure cast-on edge is not twisted and working in rnds (RS always facing), work k1 A, p1 B bicolour rib for 5 rnds, stranding colour not in use

*N*orwegian fishing boats have paid regular visits to the harbour of my home town Stornoway ever since I can remember. For me, they conjure up strong images of bold stylised colour patterns, worked in some shade of blue and cream with an occasional splash of red. These long remembered images were my starting point for Norway, and I wanted this sweater design to match the strength of the memory.

evenly across WS of work and slipping marker on each rnd.
Reading chart A from right to left, set rib and chart patt as follows—
Next rnd: *(K1 A, p1 B) 3 times; k1 A; working in st st, work rnd 1 of chart A over next 15 sts; (k1 A, p1 B) 3 times; rep from * to end of rnd.
Reading every chart rnd from right to left, work chart A in st st and work rem sts in rib as set until all 15 rnds of chart A have been completed.
Keeping continuity, work k1 A, p1 B bicolour rib over all sts for 5 rnds.

Inc rnd: With A, *m1, k14; rep from * to end. 300 sts.
Break off yarn A.
Change to 3¾mm (US 5) needles, join in yarn C and beg from rnd 1 of chart B, work 27 rnds of chart B, rep 12 patt sts 25 times in each rnd. Break off yarn C.
With yarn A, k 1 rnd.
Join in yarn B and set chart C patt as follows—

Chart rnd 1: Keeping marker in place to mark first st for beg of rnd and underarm seam st, *rep 24 patt sts of rnd 1 of chart C 6 times; work last 6 sts of chart as indicated*; place a st marker on RH needle to mark next st for centre of rnd and underarm seam st, then rep from * to * once more.
Cont in chart patt as set, rep 40 patt rnds, and work 42 rnds of chart C in total, so ending with an odd-numbered chart rnd facing for next rnd.

Begin Gussets
Next rnd: *With A, m1; with yarn B, k seam st; with yarn A, m1; keeping continuity of chart C, work next 149 sts in patt; rep from * once more. (The seam st and inc sts form the gussets – there are now 3 sts in each gusset which are represented in rnd 1 of gusset chart D.)
Cont to work chart C patt as set over 149 sts of front and back, AND AT THE SAME TIME beg with rnd 2 of gusset chart D, work gusset patt, inc 1 st at each side of each gusset on 4th chart rnd and every foll 3rd rnd as indicated on chart until 28 chart rnds of gusset chart have been completed (do not work rnd 29 yet) and there are 21 sts in each gusset. Break off yarns.

Begin Armhole Steeks
Keeping continuity of chart C patt on sts of front and back throughout, begin armhole steeks as follows—
Next rnd: Place first 21 sts of rnd (gusset) on a holder; keep first marker in place on RH needle to mark next st as beg of rnd, then onto RH needle cast on 6 sts using yarns A and B alternately — the first 5 sts just cast on are steek sts and the last one is an edge st; work next 149 sts in patt; remove 2nd st marker and place next 21

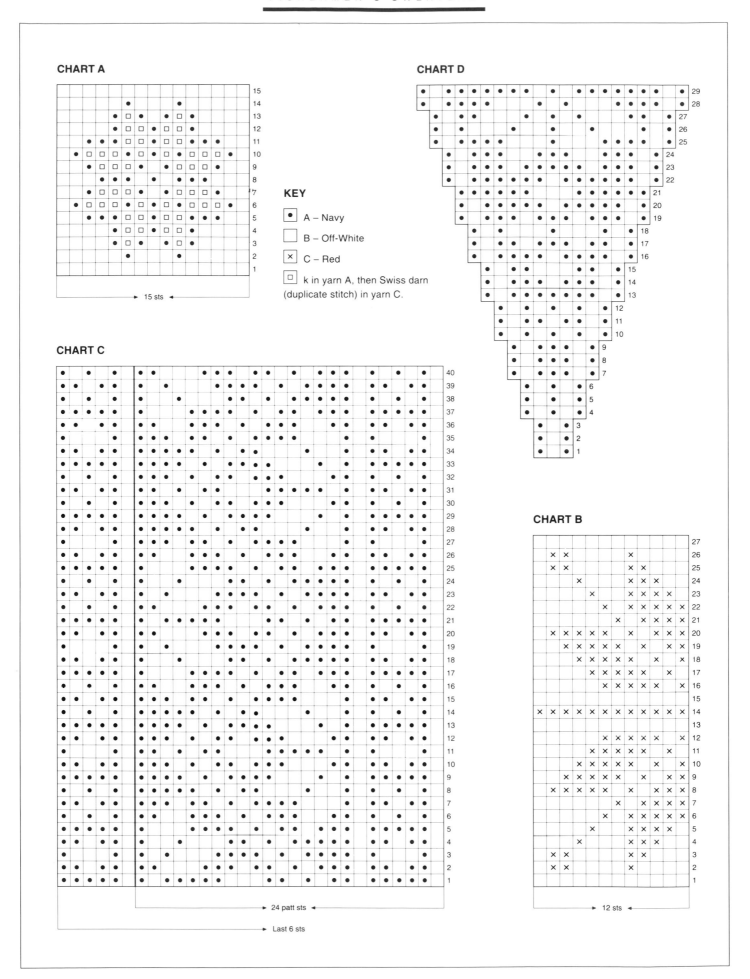

CHART A

CHART D

KEY

- • A – Navy
- ☐ B – Off-White
- ☒ C – Red
- ☐ k in yarn A, then Swiss darn (duplicate stitch) in yarn C.

15 sts

CHART C

24 patt sts

Last 6 sts

CHART B

12 sts

I chose traditional geometric patterns from the Norwegian section of my pattern library for the main body and borders of Norway. I then designed the two-colour rib with inset floral motifs and the patterned underarm gussets to further emphasise the striking nature of the design. Norway is worked in the circular Fair Isle technique, with steeks at the armholes and neck, which makes it a delightfully easy and quick design to knit. The circular Fair Isle knitting method is well worth becoming acquainted with, as it is the fastest way of knitting colour patterns. Because the entire garment is worked in the round, only knit stitches are used and the right side of the colour pattern is always facing the knitter (see page 122).

sts (gusset) on a holder; then onto RH needle cast on 12 sts using yarns A and B alternately — the first and last sts just cast on are edge sts and the centre 10 are steek sts; work next 149 sts in patt; then onto RH needle cast on 6 sts — the first st just cast on is an edge st and the last 5 are steek sts.

Working armhole steek sts in alt colours on each rnd and edge sts in yarn A throughout (see page 122 for working steeks and edge sts), cont in patt as set until 16 rnds have been worked from beg of steeks, so ending with rnd 36 of chart C inclusive.

Shape Front Neck

Next rnd: K 5 steek sts; k edge st; work next 63 sts in patt; place next 23 sts on a holder for front neck; then onto RH needle cast on 10 steek sts using yarns A and B alternately; work in patt to end of rnd.

Working all neck steek sts in alt colours on each rnd throughout, dec 1 st at each side of front neck steek on every foll rnd 7 times, then on every foll alt rnd 5 times. 51 chart C patt sts rem on each front shoulder.

Shape Back Neck

Beg back neck shaping as follows—

Next rnd: Work in patt to 149 chart patt sts of back; work next 51 sts in patt; place next 47 sts on a holder for back neck; then onto RH needle cast on 10 steek sts using yarns A and B alternately; work in patt to end of rnd.

Cont to work all neck steek sts in alt colours throughout, dec 1 st at each side of front and back neck steeks on next and foll alt rnd. 49 chart C patt sts rem on each front and back shoulder.

Work 1 rnd without shaping.

Next rnd: With alt colours, cast off first 5 steek sts of rnd; *with yarn A, k edge st; work next 49 sts in patt; with alt colours, cast off 10 front neck steek sts; work next 49 sts in patt; with yarn A, k edge st*; with alt colours, cast off next 10 steek sts; rep from * to * once; with alt colours cast off last 5 steek sts of rnd. Break off yarns.

SLEEVES

Before beg sleeves, join shoulders and prepare armhole edges as follows—

With yarn A, graft front and back shoulder and edge sts tog. (See page 121 for grafting.)

With yarn A, work backstitch up centre of first and last armhole steek sts. Cut open armhole steeks up centre, between 5th and 6th steek sts.

Begin Sleeve

With RS facing, 3¾mm (US 5) needles and yarns A and B, work rnd 29 of gusset chart D across 21 sts of gusset; break off yarn B, and with yarn A, pick up and k 126 sts evenly around armhole edge to complete rnd, working into loop of edge st next to chart patt. 147 sts.

Place a st marker on RH needle to mark beg of rnd and working in rnds, join in yarn B and set patt as follows—

Next rnd: Turn gusset chart D upside down and work chart rnd 28 across 21 gusset sts; rep 24 patt sts of rnd 36 of chart C 5 times; work last 6 sts of chart C as indicated.

Shape Gusset

Keeping continuity of chart patts as set, beg shaping gussets as follows—

Next rnd: Ssk; work centre 17 gusset sts in patt; k2tog; work in patt to end of rnd.

Cont as set, rep all rnds of charts, and dec 1 st at each side of gusset on every foll 3rd rnd until 3 gusset sts rem. 129 sts.

Work 2 rnds in patt as set without shaping.

Next rnd: With B, sl 1-k2tog-psso; work in patt to end of rnd.

Next rnd: With B, k1 (seam st); work in patt to end of rnd.

Shape Lower Sleeve

Keeping continuity of chart patts as set on sleeve sts and working seam st in yarn B throughout, work 1 rnd without shaping, then dec 1 st at each side of seam st on next and every foll 3rd rnd until 86 rnds of chart C have been worked from beg of sleeve, so ending with rnd 1 of chart C inclusive.

Next rnd: With yarn B, k seam st; with yarn A, k to end of rnd.

Break off yarn A.

Join in yarn C and beg from rnd 1 of chart B, work patt from chart B, AND AT THE SAME TIME cont to dec on every 3rd rnd until 73 sts rem, then work without shaping until all 27 rnds of chart B have been completed.

Break off yarn C.

Cuff

Dec rnd: With yarn A, (k1, k2tog) twice; *k2, k2tog; rep from * to last 3 sts; k1; k2tog. 54 sts.

Change to 3¼mm (US 3) needles and work p1 B, k1 A bicolour rib for 3 rnds. Set rib and chart A patt as follows—

Next rnd: (P1 B, k1 A) 10 times; working in st st, work rnd 1 of chart A over next 15 sts; (k1 A, p1 B) 9 times; k1 A.

Work chart A in st st and work rem sts in rib as set until all 15 rnds of chart A have been completed.

Keeping continuity of rib, work p1 B, k1 A bicolour rib over all sts (including chart A sts) for 3 rnds.

With alt colours, cast off knitwise.

NECKBAND

Before beg neckband, prepare neck edges as follows—

With yarn A, work backstitch up centre of first and last front and back neck steek sts. Cut open neck steeks up centre, between 5th and 6th steek sts.

Begin Neckband

With RS facing, 3¾mm (US 5) needles and yarn A, place first st on back neck holder on a safety pin; k rem 46 sts from back neck holder; pick up and k 5 sts evenly up left side of back neck to shoulder seam, working into chart patt st next to steek st; pick up and k 20 sts evenly down left side of front neck, working into chart patt st next to steek st; k 23 sts from front neck holder; pick up and k 20 sts evenly up right side of front neck to shoulder seam, working into st as left side; pick up and k 5 sts evenly down right side of back neck, working into st as left side; k st from safety pin. 120 sts.

Place a st marker on RH needle to mark beg of rnd and working in rnds, join in yarn B and work k1 A, p1 B bicolour rib for 2 rnds.

Set rib and chart A patt as follows—

Next rnd: *(K1 A, p1 B) 7 times; k1 A; working in st st, work rnd 1 of chart A over next 15 sts; rep from * to end of rnd.

Work chart A in st st and work rem sts in rib as set until all 15 rnds of chart A have been completed.

Keeping continuity of rib, work k1 A, p1 B bicolour rib over all sts (including chart A sts) for 3 rnds.

With alt colours, cast off knitwise.

FINISHING

Trim all steeks to 3 sts and with yarn A, cross stitch steeks in position. (See page 123 for finishing steeks.)

With yarn C, work duplicate st (Swiss darning) on all chart A motifs as indicated on chart.

Darn in all loose ends.

Press lightly on WS, omitting all ribs.

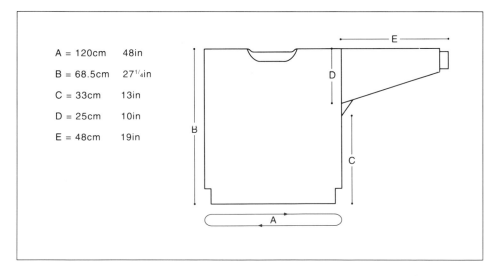

A = 120cm   48in
B = 68.5cm   27¼in
C = 33cm   13in
D = 25cm   10in
E = 48cm   19in

FAROE

SIZES

To fit medium [large]
Directions for larger size are given in brackets. Where there is only one set of figures, it applies to both sizes.

KNITTED MEASUREMENTS

Underarm, excluding gussets 116[127]cm (46½[50¾]in)
Length 67[70]cm (26½[27½]in)
Sleeve length 47[49]cm (18½[19½]in)

MATERIALS

Yarn weight used: double knitting wool (US knitting worsted)
10[11] x 50g (1¾oz) balls of Rowan *Designer DK* in A (shade no. 62 Black)
7[8] x 50g (1¾oz) balls of Rowan *Designer DK* in B (shade no. 649 Off-white)
1 set of double-pointed *or* circular 3¼mm (US 3) and 3¾mm (US 5) needles
4 stitch holders
Stitch markers

TENSION (GAUGE)

25 sts and 28 rows to 10cm (4in) measured over chart patts worked in the round (see SPECIAL NOTE), using 3¾mm (US 5) needles

SPECIAL NOTE

All charts are worked in st st.
When working a tension (gauge) swatch in chart patts, work every row on the RS only, breaking off yarns at the end of every row. (See page 123 for making a Fair Isle swatch.)

BODY

Body is worked in one piece to armhole, then steeks are added at armhole and body is cont in the rnd to shoulders.
With 3¼mm (US 3) needles and yarn A, cast on 272[296] sts.
Place a st marker on RH needle to mark beg of rnd, then making sure cast-on edge is not twisted and working in rnds (RS always facing), work k2 A, p2 B bicolour rib for 6cm (2½in), stranding colour not in

*T*he colour patterns from the Faroe Islands are very small in scale and have been traditionally used in fishermen's sweaters, either in horizontal bands or as all-over patterns. Influenced by so many of the Scottish ganseys, I decided to work these Danish motifs in vertical panels on Faroe.

use evenly across WS of work and slipping marker on each rnd.
First Size Only
Inc rnd: With A, ★m1; k16; (m1, k15) 8 times; rep from ★ once more. 290 sts.
Second Size Only
Inc rnd: With A, ★(m1, k14) 3 times; (m1, k13) 6 times; (m1, k14) twice; rep from ★ once more. 318 sts.
Both Sizes
Change to 3¾mm (US 5) needles and reading charts from right to left and beg all charts from rnd 1, set patt as follows—
Chart rnd 1: Keeping marker in place to mark first st for beg of rnd and underarm seam st, ★work chart A over first 13[18] sts; work chart B over next 11[13] sts; work chart C over next 21 sts; work chart D over next 15 sts; work chart E over

next 26 sts; work chart D over next 15 sts; work chart C over next 21 sts; work chart B over next 11[13] sts; work chart F over next 12[17] sts★; place a st marker on RH needle to mark next st for centre of rnd and underarm seam st, then rep from ★ to ★ once more.
Reading every chart rnd from right to left, cont in chart patts as set, rep all rnds of charts, until body measures 32[34]cm (12¾[13¼]in) from beg, slipping markers on every rnd throughout and ending with an odd-numbered chart rnd (on all charts) facing for next rnd.

Begin Gussets

Next rnd: ★With A, m1; k seam st; m1; keeping continuity of charts, work next 144[158] sts in patt; rep from ★ once more. (The seam st and inc sts form the gussets – there are now 3 sts in each gusset which are represented in rnd 1 of gusset chart G.)
Cont to work chart patts as set over 144[158] sts of front and back, AND AT THE SAME TIME beg with rnd 2 of gusset chart G, work gusset patt, inc 1 st at each side of each gusset on 4th chart rnd and every foll 3rd rnd as indicated on chart until 28 chart rnds of gusset chart G have been completed (do not work rnd 29 yet) and there are 21 sts in each gusset. Break off yarns.

Begin Armhole Steeks

Keeping continuity of chart patts on 144[158] sts of front and back throughout, begin armhole steeks as follows—
Next rnd: Place first 21 sts of rnd (gusset) on a holder; keep first marker in place on RH needle to mark next st as beg of rnd, then onto RH needle cast on 6 sts using yarns A and B alternately — the first 5 sts just cast on are steek sts and the last one is an edge st; work next 144[158] sts in patt; remove 2nd st marker and place next 21 sts (gusset) on a holder; then onto RH needle cast on 12 sts using yarns A and B alternately — the first and last sts just cast on are edge sts and the centre 10 are steek sts; work next 144[158] sts in patt; then onto RH needle cast on 6 sts using yarns A and B alternately — the first st just cast on is an edge st and the last 5 are steek sts.

CHART A : FIRST SIZE

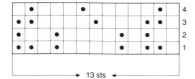

→ 13 sts ←

CHART A : SECOND SIZE

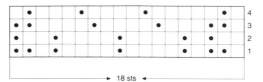

→ 18 sts ←

CHART C

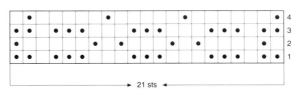

→ 21 sts ←

CHART B

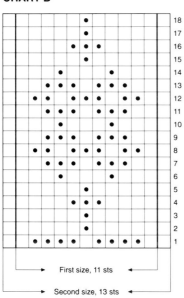

First size, 11 sts

Second size, 13 sts

CHART E

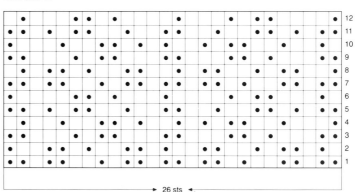

→ 26 sts ←

CHART D

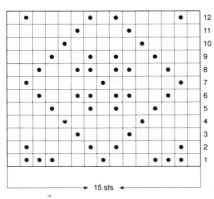

→ 15 sts ←

CHART F : FIRST SIZE

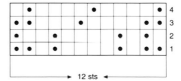

→ 12 sts ←

CHART F : SECOND SIZE

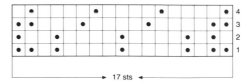

→ 17 sts ←

KEY

☐ A – Black

▪ B – Off-White

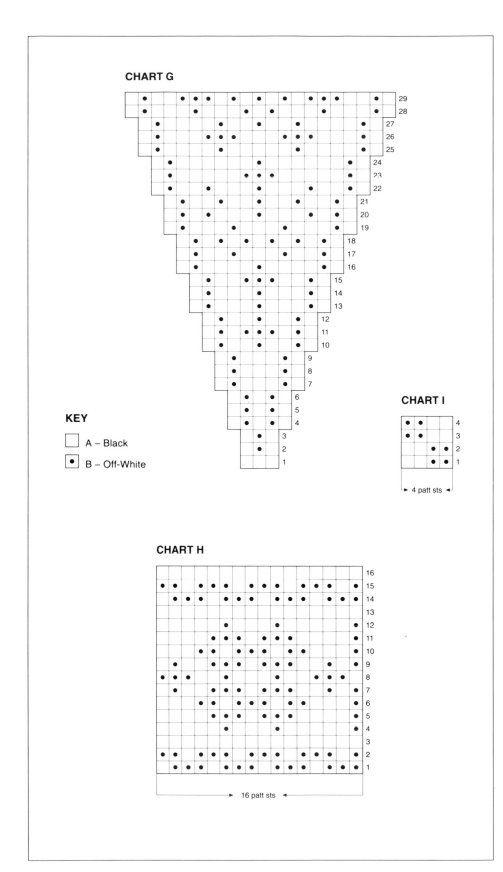

CHART G

KEY

☐ A – Black

▣ B – Off-White

CHART I

← 4 patt sts →

CHART H

← 16 patt sts →

Working armhole steek sts in alt colours on each rnd and edge sts in yarn A throughout (see page 122 for working steeks and edge sts), cont in patt as set until steeks measure 17[18]cm (6¾[7¼]in).

Shape Front Neck

Next rnd: K 5 steek sts; k edge st; work next 61[68] sts in patt; place next 22 sts on a holder for front neck; then onto RH needle cast on 10 steek sts using yarns A and B alternately; work in patt to end of rnd.

Working all neck steek sts in alt colours on each rnd throughout, dec 1 st at each side of front neck steek on every foll rnd 7 times, then on every foll alt rnd 7 times. 47[54] chart patt sts rem on each front shoulder.

Next rnd: With alt colours, cast off first 5 steek sts of rnd; k edge st; work next 47[54] sts in patt; with alt colours, cast off 10 front neck steek sts; work next 47[54] sts in patt; k edge st; with alt colours, cast off next 10 steek sts; k edge st; work next 144[158] sts in patt; k edge st; with alt colours cast off last 5 steek sts of rnd. Break off yarns.

SLEEVES

Before beg sleeves, join shoulders and prepare armhole edges as follows—
Place 50 centre back sts on a holder for back neck, and with yarn A, graft front and back shoulder and edge sts tog. (See page 121 for grafting.)
With yarn A, work backstitch up centre of first and last armhole steek sts. Cut open armhole steeks up centre, between 5th and 6th steek sts.

Begin Sleeve

With RS facing, 3¾mm (US 5) needles and yarns A and B, work rnd 29 of gusset chart G across 21 sts of gusset; break off yarn B, and with yarn A, pick up and k 122[128] sts evenly around armhole edge to complete rnd, working into loop of edge st next to chart patt. 143[149] sts. Place a st marker on RH needle to mark beg of rnd and working in rnds, join in yarn B and beg all charts (but gusset chart G) from chart rnd 1, set patt as follows—
Next rnd: Turn gusset chart G upside

down and work chart rnd 28 across 21 gusset sts; with yarn A, k1[2]; work chart B over next 11[13] sts; work chart C over next 21 sts; work chart D over next 15 sts; work chart E over next 26 sts; work chart D over next 15 sts; work chart C over next 21 sts; work chart B over next 11[13] sts; with yarn A, k1[2].

Shape Gusset

Keeping continuity of chart patts as set, beg shaping gussets as follows—

Next rnd: Ssk; work centre 17 gusset sts in patt; k2tog; work in patt to end of rnd. Cont at set, rep all rnds of charts, and dec 1 st at each side of gusset on every foll 3rd rnd until 3 gusset sts rem. 125[131] sts. Work 2 rnds in patt as set without shaping.

Next rnd: With A, sl 1-k2tog-psso; work in patt to end of rnd.

Next rnd: With A, k1 (seam st); work in patt to end of rnd.

Shape Lower Sleeve

Keeping continuity of chart patts as set on sleeve sts and working seam st in yarn A throughout, work 1 rnd without shaping, then dec 1 st at each side of seam st on next and every foll 3rd rnd until 69[73] sts rem.

Work without shaping until sleeve measures 41[43]cm (16[17]in).

Cuff

Dec rnd: With yarn A, k1[3]; *k2tog, k2; rep from * to last 0[2] sts; k0[2]. 52[56] sts.

Change to 3¼mm (US 3) needles and work k2 A, p2 B bicolour rib as body for 6cm (2½in).

Break off yarn B, and with yarn A, cast off knitwise.

NECKBAND

Before beg neckband, prepare neck edges as follows—

With yarn A, work backstitch up centre of first and last front neck steek sts. Cut open neck steek up centre, between 5th and 6th steek sts.

Begin Neckband

With RS facing, 3¼mm (US 5) needles and yarn A, k 50 sts from back neck holder; pick up and k 20 sts evenly down left side of front neck, working into chart patt st next to first steek st; k 22 sts from front neck holder; pick up and k 20 sts evenly up right side of front neck to complete rnd, working into chart patt st next to last steek st. 112 sts.

Place a st marker on RH needle to mark beg of rnd and working in rnds, join in yarn B and beg from rnd 1 of chart H, work 16 rnds of chart H, rep 16 patt sts 7 times in each rnd.

Break off yarn B and with yarn A, k 1 rnd, p 1 rnd, k 1 rnd.

Join in yarn B and beg from rnd 1 of chart I, work 4 rnds of chart I, rep 4 patt sts 28 times in each rnd. Rep 4 patt rnds 4 times in all.

Break off yarn B, and with yarn A, cast off knitwise.

*T*o counter-balance the small scale of the patterns, I worked Faroe in black and cream. Patterned underarm gussets, coloured ribs and a patterned neckband provide the ornamental touches.

FINISHING

Fold neckband in half to inside at purl rnd and sew cast-off edge in position around neckband pick up line.

Trim all steeks to 3 sts and with yarn A, cross stitch steeks in position. (See page 123 for finishing steeks.)

Darn in all loose ends.

Press lightly on WS, omitting all ribs.

A = 116[127]cm	46½[50¾]in	
B = 67[70]cm	26½[27½]in	
C = 32[34]cm	12¾[13¼]in	
D = 25[26]cm	9¾[10¼]in	
E = 47[49]cm	18½[19½]in	

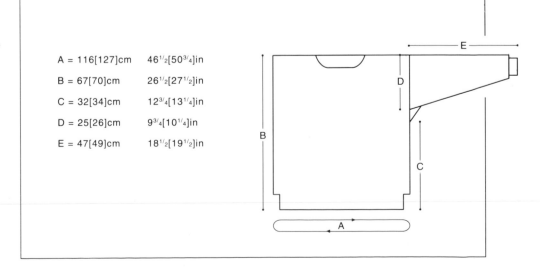

BALTIC

RATING ★

SIZES
To fit medium [large]
Directions for larger size are given in brackets.
Where there is only one set of figures, it applies
to both sizes.

KNITTED
MEASUREMENTS
Underarm 108[120]cm (43¼[48]in)
Length 68[70]cm (26¾[27½]in)
Sleeve length 44[45]cm (17½[18]in)

MATERIALS
Yarn weight used: Aran weight pure
wool yarn
10[11] x 100g (3½oz) hanks of Rowan
Magpie in A (shade no. 507 'Cloud')
1 x 100g (3½oz) hank of Rowan *Magpie* in
B (shade no. 612 'Neptune')
1 set of double-pointed *or* circular 4mm
(US 6) and 4½mm (US 7) needles
A 5mm (US 8) needle
6 stitch holders
2 safety pins
Stitch markers

TENSION (GAUGE)
20 sts and 28 rows to 10cm (4in)
measured over chart B patt, using 4½mm
(US 7) needles

SPECIAL NOTE
Charts A and C are worked in st st, using
yarns A and B. Chart B is worked using
yarn A only.

BODY
Body is worked in one piece to armhole.
With 4mm (US 6) needles and yarn A,
cast on 216[240] sts.
Place a st marker on RH needle to mark
beg of rnd, then making sure cast-on edge
is not twisted and working in rnds (RS
always facing), p 1 rnd.
Slipping marker on each rnd, join in yarn
B and work border as follows—
★★Rnd 1: ★K2 A; k2 B; rep from ★ to
end of rnd.
Rnd 2: ★P2 A; p2 B; then rep from ★ to
end of rnd.

*O*n a visit to a museum in
Helsinki in 1978, I saw an
old sweater which was labelled as a
fisherman's tunic from an unspecified
Baltic country. It is the only fishing
sweater I have seen that featured both
textured and coloured patterns.
Baltic, *with its colour-patterned trims*
and textured body, is based on this
effective idea.

Rnd 3: With yarn A, k to end of rnd.
Rnd 4: With yarn A, p to end of rnd.★★
With yarns A and B and reading every
chart rnd from right to left, set chart A
patt as follows—
Chart A rnd 1: With yarn B, k to end
of rnd.
First Size Only
Chart A rnd 2: Beg at 7th st of rnd 2 of
chart A and work last 18 sts of rep over
first 18 sts of rnd; rep 24 patt sts 8 times;
work first 6 sts of rep over last 6 sts of rnd.
Second Size Only
Chart A rnd 2: Rep 24 patt sts of rnd 2
of chart A 10 times in rnd.

Both Sizes
Cont in chart A patt as set until all 21 rnds
of chart A have been completed.
With yarn A, p 1 rnd.
With yarns A and B, work 4 rnds of
border as before from ★★ to ★★.
Break off yarn B.
Change to 4½mm (US 7) needles and
using yarn A only, set chart B patt as
follows—
Chart B rnd 1: Rep 12 patt sts of rnd 1
of chart B 18[20] times.
Cont in chart B patt as set, rep 12 patt
rnds, until body measures 43.5[44.5]cm
(17[17¼]in) from beg, ending after
working an even-numbered chart rnd.
Divide for Yokes
Next rnd: P first st of rnd and place this
st on a safety pin; keeping continuity,
work next 107[119] sts in patt; p next st
and place this st on a safety pin; turn,
leaving rem sts on a spare needle.
Front Yoke
Reading chart B from left to right for WS
(even-numbered) rows and from right to
left for RS (odd-numbered) rows, beg
with a WS row and working back and
forth in rows and keeping continuity of
patt, work 107[119] sts of front yoke in
patt until front yoke measures 16[17]cm
(6¼[6¾]in), ending with RS facing for
next row.
Shape Front Neck
Next row (RS): Keeping continuity of
patt, work 45[51] sts in patt; place next
17 sts on a holder; turn, leaving rem sts on
a spare needle.
Keeping continuity of patt throughout,
shape left side of neck as follows—
★★★Dec 1 st at neck edge on next and
every foll alt row 11 times in all.
34[40] sts rem.
Work 2 rows without shaping.
Place sts on a holder.★★★
With RS facing, rejoin yarn to 45[51] sts
of right side of neck and keeping
continuity, work 1 row without shaping,
then shape as left side of front neck from
★★★ to ★★★.
Back Yoke
With WS facing, rejoin yarn to 107[119]
sts of back yoke and keeping continuity,

CHART A

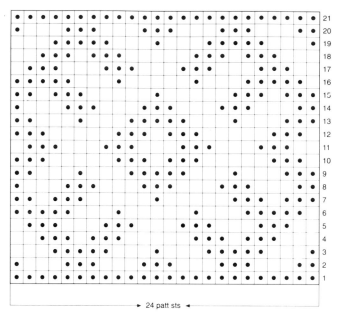

→ 24 patt sts ←

CHART B

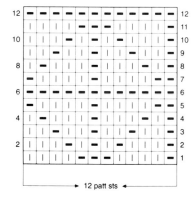

→ 12 patt sts ←

CHART C

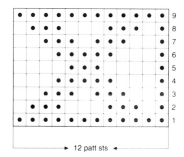

→ 12 patt sts ←

KEY

☐ A – Cloud

▣ B – Neptune

☐ k on RS rows; p on WS rows.

⊟ p on RS rows; k on WS rows.

work back and forth in rows until there are same number of rows as front to shoulders.

Place 34[40] sts at each side on holders and place 39 centre sts on a holder for back neck.

SLEEVES

Before beg sleeves, join back and front at shoulders as follows—

With 5mm (US 8) needle and yarn A, holding RS of back and front tog and with WS facing, cast off shoulder sts tog. (See page 121 for instructions for casting off sts tog.)

Begin Sleeve

With RS facing, 4½mm (US 7) needles and yarn A, p st from safety pin; pick up and k 95[99] sts evenly around armhole edge to complete rnd. 96[100] sts.

Place a st marker on RH needle to mark beg of rnd and working in rnds, set chart B patt as follows—

Chart B rnd 1: P1 (seam st); work last 5[1] sts of rep of rnd 1 of chart B over next 5[1] sts; rep 12 patt sts 7[8] times; work first 6[2] sts of rep over last 6[2] sts of rnd.

Cont to p seam st throughout and keeping continuity, work 3 rnds in chart B patt as set.

Shape Sleeve

Next rnd: P1 (seam st); k2tog; keeping continuity, work in patt to last 2 sts; ssk. Keeping continuity, cont in patt, dec 1 st at each side of seam st on every foll 5th rnd until 58[62] sts rem, then on every foll 4th rnd until 54[56] sts rem.

Cuff

Dec rnd: (K2tog, k7[5]) 6[8] times. 48 sts rem.

Change to 4mm (US 6) needles and p 1 rnd.

Join in yarn B and work 4 rnds of border as body from ★★ to ★★.

With yarns A and B, work 9 rnds of chart C, rep 12 patt sts 4 times in each rnd. With yarn A, p 1 rnd.

Work 4 rnds of border as body from ★★ to ★★.

Break off yarn B and with yarn A, cast off all sts knitwise.

NECKBAND

With RS facing, 4mm (US 6) needles and yarn A, beg at back neck and k 39 sts from back neck holder; pick up and k 20 sts evenly down left side of front neck; k 17 sts from front neck holder; pick up and k 20 sts evenly up right side of front neck to complete rnd. 96 sts.

Place a st marker on RH needle to mark beg of rnd and working in rnds (RS always facing), p 1 rnd.

Join in yarn B and work 4 rnds of border as body from ★★ to ★★.

With yarns A and B, work 9 rnds of chart C, rep 12 patt sts 8 times in each rnd.

With yarn A, p 1 rnd.

Work 4 rnds of border as body from ★★ to ★★.

Break off yarn B and with yarn A, cast off knitwise.

FINISHING

Darn in loose ends. Press Fair Isle sections gently on WS.

For this sweater I chose colour patterns from my library which typify those of several Baltic countries. I worked a small repetitive pattern in knit and purl, and bordered the design with distinctive geometric patterns from the region. The style is easy and casual, and it is worked in a heavy Aran wool. This is the perfect sweater for wild weather.

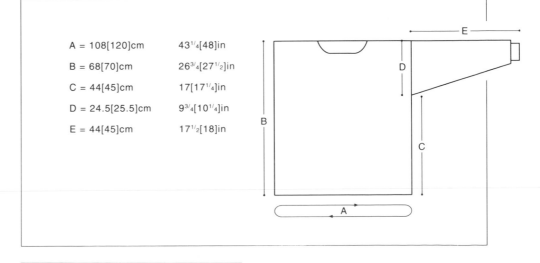

A = 108[120]cm   43¼[48]in

B = 68[70]cm   26¾[27½]in

C = 44[45]cm   17[17¼]in

D = 24.5[25.5]cm   9¾[10¼]in

E = 44[45]cm   17½[18]in

NECKBAND

With RS facing, 4mm (US 6) needles and yarn A, beg at back neck and k 39 sts from back neck holder; pick up and k 20 sts evenly down left side of front neck; k 17 sts from front neck holder; pick up and k 20 sts evenly up right side of front neck to complete rnd. 96 sts.

Place a st marker on RH needle to mark beg of rnd and working in rnds (RS always facing), p 1 rnd.

Join in yarn B and work 4 rnds of border as body from ★★ to ★★.

With yarns A and B, work 9 rnds of chart C, rep 12 patt sts 8 times in each rnd.

With yarn A, p 1 rnd.

Work 4 rnds of border as body from ★★ to ★★.

Break off yarn B and with yarn A, cast off knitwise.

FINISHING

Darn in loose ends. Press Fair Isle sections gently on WS.

For this sweater I chose colour patterns from my library which typify those of several Baltic countries. I worked a small repetitive pattern in knit and purl, and bordered the design with distinctive geometric patterns from the region. The style is easy and casual, and it is worked in a heavy Aran wool. This is the perfect sweater for wild weather.

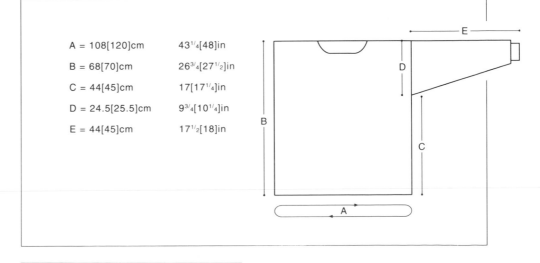

A = 108[120]cm   43¼[48]in

B = 68[70]cm   26¾[27½]in

C = 44[45]cm   17[17¼]in

D = 24.5[25.5]cm   9¾[10¼]in

E = 44[45]cm   17½[18]in

BRETON

SIZES

To fit approx age 4[6,8,10] years or 58[63,68,72]cm (23[25,27,28½]in) chest
Directions for larger sizes are given in brackets. Where there is only one set of figures, it applies to all sizes.

KNITTED MEASUREMENTS

Underarm, excluding gussets 65[70,75, 80]cm (26[28,30,32]in)
Length 38.5[42,45,48]cm (15½[16¾,18, 19¼]in)
Sleeve length 30[33,36,39]cm (12[13, 14¼,15½]in)

MATERIALS

Yarn weight used: 4-ply wool and cotton (US sport)
3[3,4,4] x 50g (1¾oz) balls of Rowan *Wool and Cotton* in A (shade no. 925 'Hibiscus')
2[2,3,3] x 50g (1¾oz) balls of Rowan *Wool and Cotton* in B (shade no. 908 'Natural')
1 set of double-pointed *or* circular 2¾mm (US 2) and 3¼mm (US 3) needles
8 stitch holders
Stitch markers
6 buttons

TENSION (GAUGE)

28 sts and 36 rows to 10cm (4in) measured over st st, using 3¼mm (US 3) needles

BODY

Body is worked in one piece to armhole.
With 2¾mm (US 2) needles and yarn A, cast on 172[184,196,208] sts.
Place a st marker on RH needle to mark beg of rnd, then making sure cast-on edge is not twisted and working in rnds (RS always facing), join in yarn B and work k2 A, p2 B bicolour rib for 5[5,6,6]cm (2[2,2½,2½]in), slipping marker on each rnd and stranding colour not in use evenly across WS of work.

First Size Only
Inc rnd: *M1; k18; (m1, k17) 4 times;

*C*lean nautical stripes are the hallmark of the fishing sweaters from the coast of Brittany. Breton is a great design for a child, with its neat underarm gussets and buttoned shoulders. Old navy uniform buttons from an Army & Navy store put the final gloss on the breezy image.

rep from * once more. 182 sts.
Second Size Only
Inc rnd: *M1; k16; (m1, k15) 4 times; m1; k16; rep from * once more. 196 sts.
Third and Fourth Sizes Only
Inc rnd: *M1; k14[13]; rep from * to end of rnd. 210[224] sts.
All Sizes
Change to 3¼mm (US 3) needles and k 4 rnds in yarn A, then k 4 rnds in yarn B. Rep these 8 rnds for stripe patt and work 39[43,47,51] rnds of stripe patt in total.
Begin Gussets
Keeping continuity of stripe patt and slipping markers on every rnd throughout, beg gussets as follows—
Next rnd: Keeping marker in place to

mark beg of rnd, *m1; k1 (seam st); m1; k90[97,104,111]*; place a st marker on RH needle to mark beg of 2nd gusset, rep from * to * once more. (The seam st and inc sts form the gussets – there are now 3 sts in each gusset.)
Cont working in st st in stripe patt, inc 1 st at at each side of each gusset on every foll 4th rnd until there are 13[15,15,17] sts in each gusset. 206[224,238,256] sts.
Divide for Yokes
Place first 13[15,15,17] sts of rnd (gusset) on a holder, leave next 90[97,104,111] sts (front yoke sts) on a spare needle, place next 13[15,15,17] sts (gusset) on a holder. 90[97,104,111] sts of back yoke rem.
Back Yoke
Beg with a WS (p) row and keeping continuity of stripe patt throughout, work 90[97,104,111] sts of back yoke in st st (p on WS rows and k on RS rows), working back and forth in rows until 53[57,61,65] rows of stripes in total have been worked from top of gussets, so ending with RS facing for next row.
Shape Back Neck
Next row (RS): K27[29,31,33]; place next 36[39,42,45] sts on a holder for back neck; turn, leaving rem sts on a spare needle.
Shape right side of neck as follows—
**Dec 1 st at neck edge on every foll row 3 times.
Place rem 24[26,28,30] sts on a holder.**
With RS facing, rejoin yarn to 27[29, 31,33] sts of left side of neck, and work 1 row without shaping, then shape as right side of neck from ** to **.
Front Yoke
With WS facing, rejoin yarn to 90[97, 104,111] sts of front yoke, and beg with a WS (p) row and keeping continuity of stripe patt, work sts of front yoke in st st, working back and forth in rows until 41[45,47,51] rows of stripes in total have been worked from top of gussets, so ending with RS facing for next row.
Shape Front Neck
Next row (RS): K39[41,45,47]; place next 12[15,14,17] sts on a holder for front neck; turn, leaving rem sts on a spare needle.

Shape left side of neck as follows—
★★★Dec 1 st at neck edge on every foll row 15[15,17,17] times.
Place rem 24[26,28,30] sts of left side of neck on a holder.★★★
With RS facing, rejoin yarn to 39[41, 45,47] sts of right side of neck, and work 1 row without shaping, then shape as left side of neck from ★★★ to ★★★.

BACK NECKBAND
With RS facing, 3¼mm (US 3) needles and yarn B, k 24[26,28,30] sts from right back shoulder holder; pick up and k 3 sts evenly down right side of back neck to back neck holder; k 36[39,42,45] sts from back neck holder, dec 0[1,0,1] st at centre back; pick up and k 3 sts evenly up left side of back neck to left shoulder holder; k 24[26,28,30] sts from left shoulder holder.
90[96,104,110] sts.
Join in yarn A and work bicolour rib as follows—
★★**Row 1 (WS):** P2[1,1,2] A; ★k2 B; p2 A; rep from ★ to last 4[3,3,4] sts; k2 B; p2[1,1,2] A.
Row 2: K2[1,1,2] A; ★p2 B; k2 A; rep from ★ to last 4[3,3,4] sts; p2 B; k2[1,1,2] A.★★★
Rep last 2 rows until neckband measures 2.5cm (1in), ending with RS facing for next row.
Break off yarn B and with yarn A, cast off all sts knitwise.

FRONT NECKBAND
With RS facing, 3¼mm (US 3) needles and yarn B, k 24[26,28,30] sts from left front shoulder holder; pick up and k 15[15,17, 17] sts evenly down left side of front neck to front neck holder; k 12[15,14,17] sts from front neck holder, dec 0[1,0,1] st at centre front; pick up and k 15[15,17,17] sts evenly up right side of front neck to right shoulder holder; k 24[26,28,30] sts from right shoulder holder.
90[96,104,110] sts.
Join in yarn A and work bicolour rib as back neckband from ★★ to ★★★ twice.
Keeping continuity of bicolour rib patt as set throughout, beg buttonholes as follows—
Buttonhole row 1 (WS): Rib 6[4,6,4]; (cast off 2, rib 6[8,8,10] including st already on needle after cast off) twice; cast off 2; rib 42[44,48,50]; (cast off 2, rib 6[8,8,10]) twice; cast off 2; rib 6[4,6,4].
Buttonhole row 2: Work in rib, casting on 2 sts over those cast off.
Work without shaping until there are same number of rows as back neckband, ending with RS facing for next row.
Break off yarn B and with yarn A, cast off knitwise.

SLEEVES
Before beg sleeves, place WS of front neckband on top of RS of back neckband at armhole edges, so that cast-off edge of front is directly on top of pick up row of

back neckband, and pin in this position.
Begin Sleeve
With RS facing, 3¼mm (US 3) needles and yarn B[B,A,A], k 13[15,15,17] sts from gusset holder; pick up and k 94[100,106,112] sts evenly around armhole edge to complete rnd, picking up sts through both front and back neckband when reached, thus joining them tog.
107[115,121,129] sts.
Shape Gusset
Place a st marker on RH needle to mark beg of rnd and working in rnds (RS always facing), beg shaping gusset as follows—
Next rnd: With yarn B[B,A,A], ssk; k9[11,11,13]; k2tog; k to end of rnd.
With yarn B[B,A,A], k 2 rnds without shaping.
Join in yarn A[A,B,B] and k 1 rnd more without shaping.
Then working in st st in stripe patt as body throughout, dec 1 st at each side of gusset on next and every foll 4th rnd until 3 gusset sts rem. 97[103,109,115] sts.
Work 3 rnds without shaping.
Next rnd: Sl 1-k2tog-psso; k to end of rnd.
Next rnd: K1 (seam st); k to end of rnd.
Work 1[1,2,2] rnds more without shaping.
Shape Lower Sleeve
Beg shaping lower sleeve as follows—
Next rnd: K1 (seam st); k2tog; k to last 2 sts; ssk.

A = 65[70,75,80]cm	26[28,30,32]in
B = 38.5[42,45,48]cm	15½[16¾,18,19¼]in
C = 16[17,19,20]cm	6¼[6¾,7¾,8]in
D = 16[17,18,19]cm	6¼[6¾,7¼,7½]in
E = 30[33,36,39]cm	12[13,14¼,15½]in

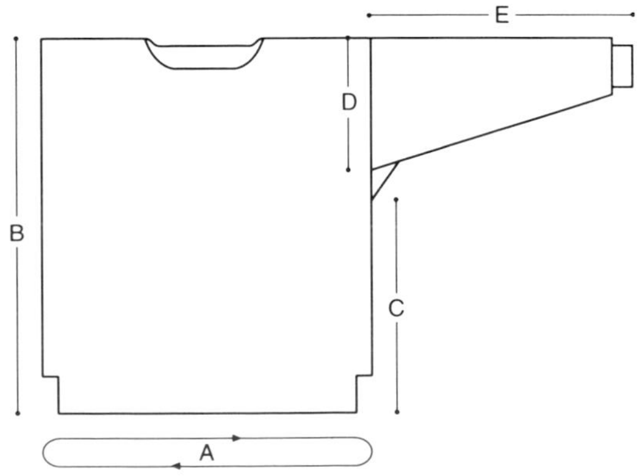

Work 2[2,3,3] rnds without shaping.
First and Second Sizes Only
Dec 1 st at each side of seam st on next rnd and then on every foll 3rd rnd until 53[57] sts rem.
Work 4[7] rnds without shaping.
Third and Fourth Sizes Only
Dec 1 st at each side of seam st on next and every foll 4th rnd until 69 sts rem, then on every foll 3rd rnd until 63[67] sts rem.

Cuff: All Sizes
Dec rnd: (K2tog, k4[5,4,5]) 4[2,4,1] times; (k2tog, k3[4,3,4]) 1[6,3,9] times; (k2tog, k4[5,4,4]) 4[1,4,1] times. 44[48,52,56] sts.
Change to 2¾mm (US 2) needles and work k2 A, p2 B bicolour rib until sleeve measures 30[33,36,39]cm (12[13,14¼, 15½]in).
Break off yarn B and with yarn A, cast off knitwise.

*B*ecause it is worked in simple stocking stitch stripes, Breton is an ideal project if you are looking for a quick and easy exercise in the circular gansey technique.

FINISHING
Darn in loose ends. Press garment gently on WS, omitting ribs. Sew on buttons.

NEW WORLD

This metaphorical journey concludes in the New World.
My aim was to create designs that take a fresh
look at the tradition of fishermen's sweaters and that
take my favourite features in new directions.

MYSTIC

RATING ★ ★ ★

SIZES

To fit small [medium, large]
Directions for larger sizes are given in brackets.
Where there is only one set of figures, it applies
to all sizes.

KNITTED MEASUREMENTS

Underarm 110[117,124]cm (44[46½, 49]in)
Length 76.5[79,81.5]cm (30½[31½,32¼]in)
Sleeve length 53[54,55]cm (21[21¼, 21¾]in)

WASHED MEASUREMENTS

Underarm 110[117,124]cm 44[46½,49]in)
Length 66.5[69,71.5]cm (26½[27½,28¼]in)
Sleeve length 46[47,48]cm (18[18¼,18½]in)

MATERIALS

Yarn weight used: indigo dyed unshrunk double knitting cotton (US medium weight cotton)
24[25,26] x 50g (1¾oz) balls of Rowan *Den-m-nit Cotton DK* in shade no. 225 'Nashville'
1 pair each 3¼mm (US 3) and 3¾mm (US 5) needles
1 cable needle
Stitch markers

TENSION (GAUGE)

24 sts and 30 rows to 10cm (4in) measured over chart A patt (before washing), using 3¾mm (US 5) needles

SPECIAL NOTE

Rowan *Den-m-nit Indigo Dyed Cotton DK* will shrink and fade when washed. When washed for the first time the yarn will shrink by up to one fifth in length, but the width with remain the same. This sweater is specially designed for this yarn and all the necessary adjustments have been made in the instructions to obtain the washed measurements listed above. To make an accurate swatch, cast on 33 sts and work the patt from chart A,

A voyage to the New World calls for a look at some new horizons. Mystic takes old gansey and Aran stitch patterns and juxtaposes them in a new way. In tune with this combination of old and new, I chose the anchor as my main motif.

repeating the 8 patt sts 4 times, then work the last st as indicated on chart.

BACK

**With 3¼mm (US 3) needles, cast on 122[128,134] sts.
Work k1, p1 rib for 8[9,10]cm (3¼[3½, 4]in).
Inc row (WS): Keeping continuity of rib, rib 7[4,1]; *m1, rib 6; rep from * to last 7[4,1] sts; m1; rib 7[4,1].
141[149,157] sts.
Change to 3¾mm (US 5) needles and reading charts from right to left for RS (odd-numbered) rows and from left to right for WS (even-numbered) rows and beg all charts from row 1, set chart patts as follows—

Chart row 1 (RS): Work chart A over first 17[21,25] sts, working first 0[4,0] sts of chart as indicated, rep 8 patt sts 2[2,3] times and working last st of chart as indicated; work chart B over next 7 sts; work chart C over next 23 sts; work chart D over next 7 sts; work chart E over next 12 sts; work chart F over next 9 sts; work chart E over next 12 sts; work chart B over next 7 sts; work chart C over next 23 sts; work chart D over next 7 sts; work chart G over last 17[21,25] sts, rep 8 patt sts 2[2,3] times and working last 1[5,1] sts of chart as indicated.**
Cont in patts as set, rep all rows of each chart until 200 rows of chart patts have been worked in total, thus working 5 reps of each chart C patt.
Second and Third Sizes Only:
Work 4[8] rows more as set, but working rev st st over 23 sts of each chart C patt.
All Sizes
Next row: Cast off 42[45,48] sts and mark last st cast off with a piece of yarn; cast off next 57[59,61] sts, dec 2 sts at each chart E and chart F cables during cast off; cast off rem 42[45,48] sts and mark first st cast off with a piece of yarn.

FRONT

Work as back from ** to **.
Cont in patts as set, rep all rows of each chart until 178[182,186] rows of chart patts have been worked in total, thus ending on row 18[22,26] inclusive of 5th rep of chart C.
Shape Front Neck
Next row (RS): Keeping continuity, work charts A, B, C, D and first 2 sts of chart E; cast off centre 29 sts, dec 2 sts at each chart E and chart F cables during cast off; turn, leaving rem sts on a spare needle.
Keeping continuity, cont in patt as set until 200 rows of chart patts have been worked in total, then work 0[4,8] rows more as set, but working rev st st over 23 sts of each chart C patt, AND AT THE SAME TIME shape left side of neck as follows—
***Cast off 2[2,3] sts at beg of next row.
Work 1 row without shaping.

CHART A

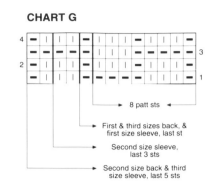

→ 8 patt sts ←

→ All sizes,
last st

Second size sleeve,
first 2 sts ←

Second size back & third →
size sleeve, first 4 sts

CHART G

→ 8 patt sts ←

→ First & third sizes back, &
first size sleeve, last st

→ Second size sleeve,
last 3 sts

→ Second size back & third
size sleeve, last 5 sts

CHART B

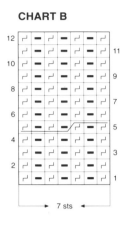

→ 7 sts ←

CHART C

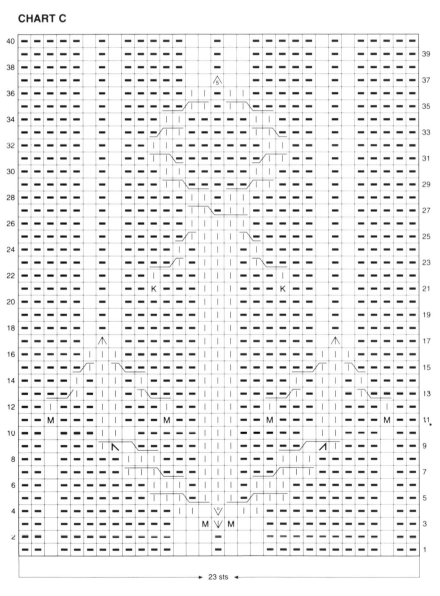

→ 23 sts ←

CHART D

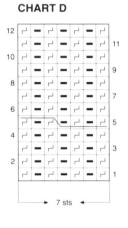

→ 7 sts ←

CHART E

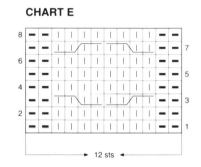

→ 12 sts ←

CHART F

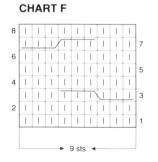

→ 9 sts ←

KEY

| | k on RS rows; p on WS rows.

| | p on RS rows; k on WS rows.

| | k into back of st on RS rows; p into back of st on WS rows.

| | no stitch.

| | sl first 2 sts to cn and hold at back; k2; k2 from cn.

| | sl first 2 sts to cn and hold at front; k2; k2 from cn.

| | sl first 3 sts to cn and hold at front; k3; k3 from cn.

| | sl first 3 sts to cn and hold at back; k3; k3 from cn.

| | sl first 4 sts to cn and hold at back; k1b, p1, k1b; p1, k1b, p1, k1b from cn.

| | sl first 3 sts to cn and hold at front; k1b, p1, k1b, p1; k1b, p1, k1b from cn.

| M | make 1 st by picking up the strand between the last st worked and the next st, and k into the back of strand.

| V | (k1b, k1) into same st, then insert left hand needle point between the vertical strand that runs down between the 2 sts just made and k into this strand, making the third st of the group.

| V | (p1, yo, p1) into same st, making 3 sts in the group.

| | sl first 2 sts to cn and hold at back; k3; p1, k1 from cn.

| | sl first 3 sts to cn and hold at front; k1, p1; k3 from cn.

| | sl first 2 sts to cn and hold at back; k3; p2 from cn.

| | sl first 3 sts to cn and hold at front; p2; k3 from cn.

| | sl first 2 sts to cn and hold at back; k1, k2tog; p2 from cn.

| | sl first 3 sts to cn and hold at front; p2; ssk, k1 from cn.

| | sl first st to cn and hold at front; p2; k1 from cn.

| | sl first 2 sts to cn and hold at back; k1; p2 from cn.

| | sl first st to cn and hold at front; p1; k1 from cn.

| | sl first st to cn and hold at back; k1; p1 from cn.

| | sl 2 sts tog knitwise; k1; pass the 2 slipped sts over the k st.

| K | make knot thus – (k1, p1) twice into same st, then sl the first 3 sts made over the last st made.

| | sl first 2 sts to cn and hold at back; k2; p2 from cn.

| | sl first 2 sts to cn and hold at front; p2; k2 from cn.

| | sl decrease 5 sts tog thus – sl 3 knitwise, one at a time, with yarn at back, drop yarn, then * pass the second st on right hand needle over the first (centre) st; sl the centre st back to left hand needle and pass the next st on left hand needle over it **; sl the centre st back to right hand needle and rep from * to ** once more; p the centre st.

| | sl first 3 sts to cn and hold at front; k2; sl the p st from cn onto left needle and p it; k2 from cn.

*I*nstead of the traditional knit and purl portrayal, I have designed the anchor motif on Mystic in a sculpted cable form and combined it with robust rope and chain cables, and a textured gansey pattern. I then arranged the patterns in the panelled Aran style. Denim yarn and cabled neckline complete the fresh and energetic mood of Mystic. The cabled collar is knit in a separate strip and when the sweater is complete, it is sewn on around the neckline. As for Filey (page 49), this gansey is designed specially for unshrunk denim yarn.

Cast off 2 sts at beg of next row.
Dec 1 st at neck edge on every foll row 6 times, then at same edge on every foll alt row 4[5,5] times. 42[45,48] sts rem.
Work without shaping until all 200[204,208] rows of chart patts have been completed as set.
Cast off all sts.★★★
With RS facing, rejoin yarn to sts of right side of neck, and keeping continuity as set for left side of neck, work 2 rows without shaping, then shape as left side of front neck from ★★★ to ★★★.

S L E E V E S

With 3¼mm (US 3) needles, cast on 46[48,50] sts.
Work k1, p1 rib for 7cm (2¾in).
Inc row (WS): K5[4,3]; (m1, k2) 18[20,22] times; m1; k5[4,3]. 65[69,73] sts.
Change to 3¾mm (US 5) needles and beg all charts from row 1, set patt as follows—
Chart row 1 (RS): Work chart A over first 9[11,13] sts, working first 0[2,4] sts of chart as indicated, working 8 patt sts once and working last st of chart as indicated; work chart B over next 7 sts; work chart E over next 12 sts; work chart F over next 9 sts; work chart E over next 12 sts; work chart D over next 7 sts; work chart G over last 9[11,13] sts, working 8 patt sts

once and working last 1[3,5] sts of chart as indicated.
Cont in patts as set, rep all rows of each chart and inc 1 st at each end of every foll 3rd row until there are 75 sts, then on every foll 4th row until there are 131[135,137] sts, working all increased sts into chart A and chart G patts.
Work in patt without shaping until sleeve measures 53[54,55]cm (21[21¼,21¾]in) from beg, ending with RS facing for next row.
Shape Saddle
Keeping continuity, cast off 59[61,62] sts at beg of next 2 rows, dec 2 sts at chart E cable during each cast off. 13 sts rem.
Keeping continuity, cont working 13 sts of saddle in patt (chart F with 2 p sts at each side) until saddle measures 20.5[22, 23.5]cm (8[8¾,9¼]in).
Cast off all sts, dec 2 sts at chart F cable during cast off.

C O L L A R

With 3¾mm (US 5) needles, cast on 33 sts.
Beg all charts from row 1, set patt as follows—
Chart row 1 (RS): Work chart E over first 12 sts; work chart F over next 9 sts; work chart E over last 12 sts.
Cont in patts as set, rep all rows of each

chart, until collar measures 62[64,65]cm (24½[25¼,25½]in).
Cast off all sts, dec 2 sts at each cable during cast off.

F I N I S H I N G

Following instructions on yarn label, wash and dry all knitted pieces, plus approx 5m (6yd) of yarn for sewing up. This will allow the garment pieces to shrink to finished size (see SPECIAL NOTE at beginning of instructions).
Place markers 24[24.5,25]cm (9½[9¾, 10]in) down from shoulder cast off at each side of back and front. Sew saddles to back and front shoulders, placing the end of the saddle at yarn markers on back, and at neck edge on front. Place each end of top of sleeve at markers on front and back, and sew sleeves to body.
Press seams lightly on WS.
With RS of collar and body facing each other, place cast-on end of collar at centre of left shoulder saddle. Pin and stitch collar around neckline, easing neckline evenly along back neck and around front neck, so that cast-off end meets cast-on end at centre of left saddle. Sew ends of collar together. Turn collar in half to the inside and slip stitch in position.
Sew up side and sleeve seams and press seams lightly on WS, omitting ribs.

Knitted Measurements

A = 55[58.5,62]cm   22[23¼,24½]in

B = 74.5[77,79.5]cm   29¾[30¾,31½]in

E = 53[54,55]cm   21[21¼,21¾]in

Washed Measurements

A = 55[58.5,62]cm   22[23¼,24½]in

B = 64.5[67,69.5]cm   25¾[26¾,27½]in

C = 41.5[43.5,44.5]cm   16¼[17,17½]in

D = 24[24.5,25]cm   9½[9¾,10]in

E = 46[47,48]cm   18[18¼,18¾]in

F = 4cm   1½in

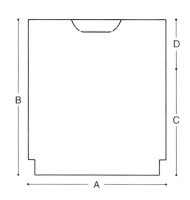

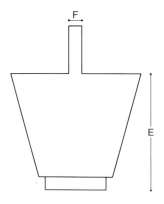

NANTUCKET

SIZES

To age 6[8,10,12] years or 63[68,72, 76]cm (25[27,28½,30]in) chest
Directions for larger sizes are given in brackets. Where there is only one set of figures, it applies to all sizes.

KNITTED MEASUREMENTS

Underarm 72[79,85,92]cm (29[31½,34, 37]in)
Length 43[47,51,55]cm (17[18½,20, 21¾]in)
Sleeve length 32[35,38,41]cm (12½[13¾, 15,16]in)

MATERIALS

Yarn weight used: Aran weight pure wool yarn
5[5,6,7] x 100g (3½oz) hanks of Rowan *Magpie* in shade no. 305 'Ocean' or 306 'Peony'
1 pair each of 4½mm (US 7) and 5mm (US 8) needles
1 set of double-pointed 4½mm (US 7) needles
1 cable needle
4 stitch holders
Stitch markers

TENSION (GAUGE)

18 sts and 24 rows to 10cm (4in) measured over Main patt, using 5mm (US 8) needles

MAIN PATTERN

To check tension (gauge) work Main patt over any number of sts as follows—
Rows 1, 3 and 5 (RS): Knit.
Rows 2, 4, 6, 7 and 8: Purl.
Rep rows 1 through 8.

BACK

★★With 4½mm (US 7) needles, cast on 59[63,67,71] sts.
Reading chart A from right to left for RS (odd-numbered) rows and from left to right for WS (even-numbered) rows, set rib and cable patt as follows—
Row 1 (RS): (P1, k1) 11[12,13,14]

My design Nantucket is another combination of the Aran and gansey patterns. I wanted to create a quick, easy and dynamic child's sweater, using just the barest elements of the two styles. A single central cable with knots – worked on a background of purl pennants and thin horizontal bars – defines the image.

times; p1; work row 1 of chart A over next 13 sts; p1; (k1, p1) 11[12,13,14] times.
Row 2: (K1, p1) 11[12,13,14] times; k1; work row 2 of chart A over next 13 sts; k1; (p1, k1) 11[12,13,14] times.
Cont in patt as set, rep 8 patt rows of chart A over centre 13 sts, and work 15 rows in total, ending with WS facing for next row.
Inc row (WS): Keeping continuity of rib, rib 2[3,2,1]; (m1, rib 5[4,4,4]) 4[5,6,7] times; m1; rib 1[2,1,0]; work row 8 of

chart A over next 13 sts; rib 1[2,1,0]; (m1, rib 5[4,4,4]) 4[5,6,7] times; m1; rib 2[3,2,1]. 69[75,81,87] sts.
Change to 5mm (US 8) needles and set patt as follows—
Patt row 1 (RS): Work row 1 of Main patt over first 23[26,29,32] sts; work row 1 of chart B over next 23 sts; work row 1 of Main patt over last 23[26,29,32] sts.★★★
Cont in patt as set, rep 8 patt rows of chart B over centre 23 sts and 8 patt rows of Main patt over rem sts until back measures 40[44,48,52]cm (15¾[17¼, 18¾,20½]in), ending with RS facing for next row.
Shape Shoulders
Cast off 19[21,23,26] sts at beg of next 2 rows.
Place rem centre 31[33,35,35] sts on a holder.

FRONT

Work as back from ★★ to ★★★.
Cont in patt as set, rep 8 patt rows of chart B over centre 23 sts and 8 patt rows of Main patt over rem sts until front measures 8[8,10,10] rows fewer than back to shoulder, ending with RS facing for next row.
Shape Front Neck
Next row (RS): Keeping continuity, work 26[28,31,34] sts in patt; place next 17[19,19,19] sts on a holder; turn, leaving rem sts on a spare needle.
Keeping continuity of patt throughout, shape left side of neck as follows—
★Cast off 2 sts at beg of next row. 24[26,29,32] sts.
Dec 1 st at neck edge on every foll row 4 times, then on every foll alt row 1[1,2,2] times, so ending with same number of rows as back to shoulder.
19[21,23,26] sts rem.
Cast off all sts.★★
With RS facing, rejoin yarn to sts of right side of neck, and keeping continuity, work 2 rows in patt without shaping, then shape as left side of neck from ★ to ★★.

SLEEVES

With 4½mm (US 7) needles, cast on 33[35,37,39] sts.

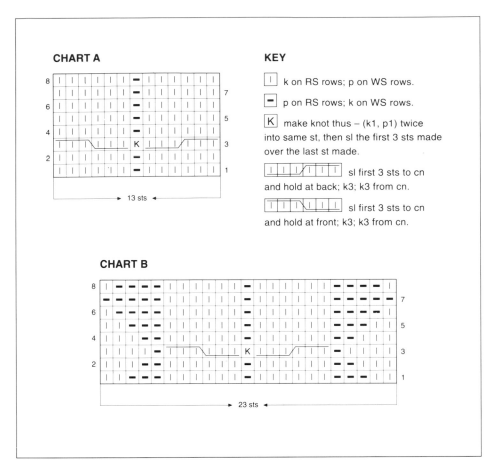

CHART A

KEY

| | k on RS rows; p on WS rows.

■ p on RS rows; k on WS rows.

K make knot thus – (k1, p1) twice into same st, then sl the first 3 sts made over the last st made.

sl first 3 sts to cn and hold at back; k3; k3 from cn.

sl first 3 sts to cn and hold at front; k3; k3 from cn.

CHART B

← 13 sts →

← 23 sts →

Beg chart A from row 1, set rib and cable patt as follows—

Row 1 (RS): P0[1,0,1]; (k1, p1) 5[5,6,6] times; work row 1 of chart A over next 13 sts; (p1, k1) 5[5,6,6] times; p0[1,0,1].

Row 2: K0[1,0,1]; (p1, k1) 5[5,6,6] times; work row 2 of chart A over next 13 sts; (k1, p1) 5[5,6,6] times; k0[1,0,1].

Cont in patt as set, rep 8 patt rows of chart A over centre 13 sts, and work 15 rows in total, ending with WS facing for next row.

Inc row (WS): Keeping continuity of rib, rib 1[1,2,1]; (m1, rib 4[5,3,4]) 2[2,3,3] times; m1; rib 1[0,1,0]; work row 8 of chart A over next 13 sts; rib 1[0,1,0]; (m1, rib 4[5,3,4]) 2[2,3,3] times; m1; rib 1[1,2,1]. 39[41,45,47] sts.

Change to 5mm (US 8) needles and set patt as follows—

Patt row 1 (RS): Work row 1 of Main patt over first 8[9,11,12] sts; work row 1 of chart B over next 23 sts; work row 1 of Main patt over last 8[9,11,12] sts.

Cont in patt as set, rep 8 patt rows of chart B over centre 23 sts and 8 patt rows of Main patt over rem sts, and inc 1 st at each end of every 3rd row until there are 57[59,59,61] sts, then on every foll 4th row until there are 73[79,85,91] sts, working all increased sts into Main patt and ending with RS facing for next row.

Shape Saddle

Cast off 29[32,35,38] sts at beg of next 2 rows.

Keeping continuity of patt, work centre 15 sts without shaping until saddle fits in length along shoulder cast-off edge.

Place sts on a holder.

FINISHING

Do not press pieces.

Place markers 16[18,19.5,21]cm (6½[7,7¾,8½]in) down from shoulder cast off at each side of back and front. Sew

*K*nitted in an Aran weight yarn, Nantucket *would be a success in any colour, and it would suit either a boy or a girl.*

saddles along shoulder cast-off edges of front and back. Place each end of top of sleeve at markers on front and back, and sew sleeves to body.

Press seams very lightly on WS.

Sew up side and sleeve seams and press seams very lightly on WS, omitting ribs.

NECKBAND

With RS facing and double-pointed 4½mm (US 7) needles, beg at back neck st holder and keeping continuity of cable patts as set throughout, pick up sts as follows—

(K9[10,11,11], dec 1[0,1,1] st at centre of this group of sts; work in patt across 13 sts of cable; k9[10,11,11], dec 1[0,1,1] st at centre of this group of sts) all from back neck holder; work 15 sts in patt from left saddle holder; pick up and k 6[7,9,9] sts evenly down left side of front neck to front neck holder; (k2[3,3,3]; work in patt across 13 sts of cable; k2[3,3,3]) all from front neck holder; pick up and k 6[7,9,9] sts evenly up right front neck to right saddle; work 15 sts in patt from right saddle holder to complete rnd. 88[96,100,100] sts.

Place a st marker on RH needle to mark beg of rnd, then working in rnds (RS always facing) and keeping continuity of chart A cable patts (reading all chart rnds from right to left), set rib and cable patt as follows—

Rnd 1: (K1, p1) 4[5,5,5] times; work in patt across 13 sts of back cable; (p1, k1) 4[5,5,5] times; p1; work in patt across 13 sts of left saddle cable; p1; (k1, p1) 4[5,6,6] times; work in patt across 13 sts of front cable; (p1, k1) 4[5,6,6] times; p1; work in patt across 13 sts of right saddle cable; p1.

Cont in patt as set until neckband measures 5cm (2in).

Next rnd: Work all rib sts in rib as set and dec across each of 13-st cables as follows — (k1, k2tog) 4 times; k1. 72[80,84,84] sts rem.

K 4 rnds.

Cast off knitwise

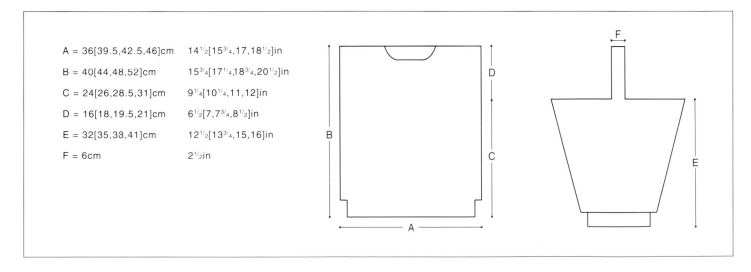

A = 36[39.5,42.5,46]cm   14½[15¾,17,18½]in

B = 40[44,48,52]cm   15¾[17¼,18¾,20½]in

C = 24[26,28.5,31]cm   9¼[10¼,11,12]in

D = 16[18,19.5,21]cm   6½[7,7¾,8½]in

E = 32[35,38,41]cm   12½[13¾,15,16]in

F = 6cm   2½in

CAPE COD

SIZE
One size fits 86-97cm (34-38in) bust

KNITTED MEASUREMENTS
Underarm, excluding gussets 107cm (42in)
Length 66cm (26in)
Sleeve length 47cm (18½in)

MATERIALS
Yarn weight used: 4-ply silk and wool (US sport)
29 x 20g (¾oz) balls of Rowan *Silk and Wool* in shade no. 851 'Camel'
1 set of double-pointed *or* circular 2¾mm (US 2) needles
1 set of double-pointed 2¼mm (US 1) needles
1 cable needle
8 stitch holders
Stitch markers

TENSION (GAUGE)
34 sts and 45 rows to 10cm (4in) measured over st st, using 2¾mm (US 2) needles (see note below)

SPECIAL NOTE
The sweater is entirely patterned throughout. The st st tension (gauge) swatch simply makes it easier to accurately measure the tension (gauge).

BODY
Body is worked in one piece to armhole.
With 2¾mm (US 2) needles, cast on 352 sts.
Place a st marker on RH needle to mark beg of rnd, then making sure cast-on edge is not twisted and working in rnds (RS always facing), set chart A border patt as follows—
Chart A rnd 1: Reading chart from right to left, rep 4 patt sts of rnd 1 of chart A 88 times.
Reading every chart rnd from right to left and slipping marker on every rnd throughout, cont in chart A patt as set and work rnds 2 through 3 once, rep rnds 4

*T*he best of the old Scottish *ganseys were beautiful examples of elaborate artistry and* Cape Cod *is an expression of my admiration for them. My pattern theme remains closely connected with the sea, but I wanted* Cape Cod *to be a distinctively feminine design in honour of the inspired knitters of the past.*

through 7 a total of 3 times, then work last 3 rnds of chart, thus working 18 rnds of chart A in total from beg.
Inc rnd: Keeping marker in place to mark first st for beg of rnd and underarm seam st, *k1 (seam st); (p2, m1, k6, m1, p2, k23) 5 times; p2; m1; k6; m1; p2*; place a st marker on RH needle to mark next st for centre of rnd and underarm seam st, then rep from * to * once more. 376 sts.
Beg with rnd 1 of chart B, set body patt as follows—

Chart B rnd 1: *K seam st; rep 35 patt sts of rnd 1 of chart B 5 times; work first 12 sts of rep over next 12 sts; rep from * once more.
Cont in chart B patt as set, rep the 32 patt rnds, until 144 chart B rnds in total have been completed, so ending with chart B rnd 16 inclusive.
Begin Gussets
Next rnd: *M1; k1; m1; keeping continuity, work 187 sts in patt (following rnd 17 of chart B); rep from * once more. (The k st and the inc sts form the gussets – there are now 3 sts in each gusset which are represented in rnd 1 of gusset chart C.)
Cont to work chart B patt as set over 187 sts of back and front, AND AT THE SAME TIME beg with rnd 2 of gusset chart C, work gusset patt, inc 1 st at each side of each gusset on 5th chart rnd and every foll 4th rnd as indicated on chart until 45 chart rnds of gusset chart have been completed (do not work rnd 46 yet) and there are 25 sts in each gusset, so ending with chart B rnd 29 inclusive. 424 sts.
Divide for Yokes
Place first 25 sts of rnd (gusset) on a holder, leave next 187 sts (front yoke sts) on a spare needle, place next 25 sts (gusset) on a holder. 187 sts of back yoke rem.
Back Yoke
Beg with a WS row and keeping continuity of patt, work 187 sts of back yoke in chart B patt, working back and forth in rows (now reading WS chart rows from left to right and RS rows from right to left) until 99 rows have been worked in total, so ending with chart B row 32 inclusive.
Dec row (RS): Keeping continuity, work first 49 sts in patt; (k2tog, k1) 3 times; k2tog; place these last 56 sts on a holder; work next 67 sts in patt and place these sts on a holder for back neck; (k2tog, k1) 3 times; k2tog; work next 49 sts in patt; place these last 56 sts on a holder.
Front Yoke
With WS facing, rejoin yarn to 187 sts of front yoke and keeping continuity, work chart B patt back and forth in rows until

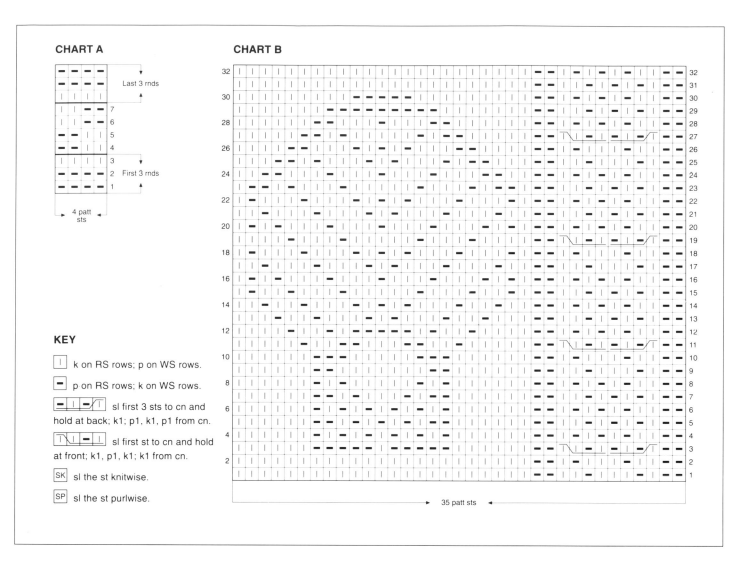

CHART A

Last 3 rnds

7
6
5
4
3
2 First 3 rnds
1

4 patt sts

KEY

| I | k on RS rows; p on WS rows. |

| − | p on RS rows; k on WS rows. |

| − I −/ | sl first 3 sts to cn and hold at back; k1; p1, k1, p1 from cn. |

| \− I | sl first st to cn and hold at front; k1, p1, k1; k1 from cn. |

| SK | sl the st knitwise. |

| SP | sl the st purlwise. |

CHART B

35 patt sts

---

75 rows have been worked in total, so ending with chart B row 8 inclusive.

Shape Front Neck

Next row (RS): Keeping continuity, work 71 sts in patt; place next 45 sts on a holder for front neck; turn, leaving rem sts on a spare needle.

Keeping continuity of patt throughout, shape left side of neck as follows—

**Dec 1 st at neck edge on next and every foll alt row 11 times in all.

60 sts rem.

Work 2 rows without shaping, so ending with chart B row 32 inclusive.**

Dec row (RS): Keeping continuity, work first 49 sts in patt; (k2tog, k1) 3 times; k2tog.

Place rem 56 sts on a holder.

With RS facing, rejoin yarn to right side of neck and keeping continuity, work 1 row without shaping, then shape as left side of neck from ★★ to ★★.

Dec row (RS): (K2tog, k1) 3 times; k2tog; work last 49 sts in patt.

Place rem 56 sts on a holder.

NECK GUSSETS

Before beg left neck gusset join back and front at shoulders as follows—

Place left back and left front shoulder sts on 2 separate double-pointed 2¼mm (US 1) needles. With 2¼mm (US 2) needle, holding WS of left back and front shoulders tog and beg at armhole edge of shoulder, cast off shoulder sts tog until 8 sts rem on each of back and front shoulder

needles at neck edge. (See page 121 for casting off sts tog.)

Left Neck Gusset

★★Keeping single st rem from shoulder cast off on 2¼mm (US 2) needle and with RS facing, set chart D patt and work gusset back and forth on 2¼mm (US 1) needles holding 8 rem back and front shoulder sts as follows—

Chart D row 1 (RS): Holding needle with 8 front shoulder sts in left hand and needle holding 8 back shoulder sts in right hand, k single st rem from shoulder cast off onto RH needle; with yarn at front, sl next st from front shoulder knitwise onto RH needle; turn.

Chart D row 2: P2; with yarn at front, sl next st from back shoulder purlwise onto

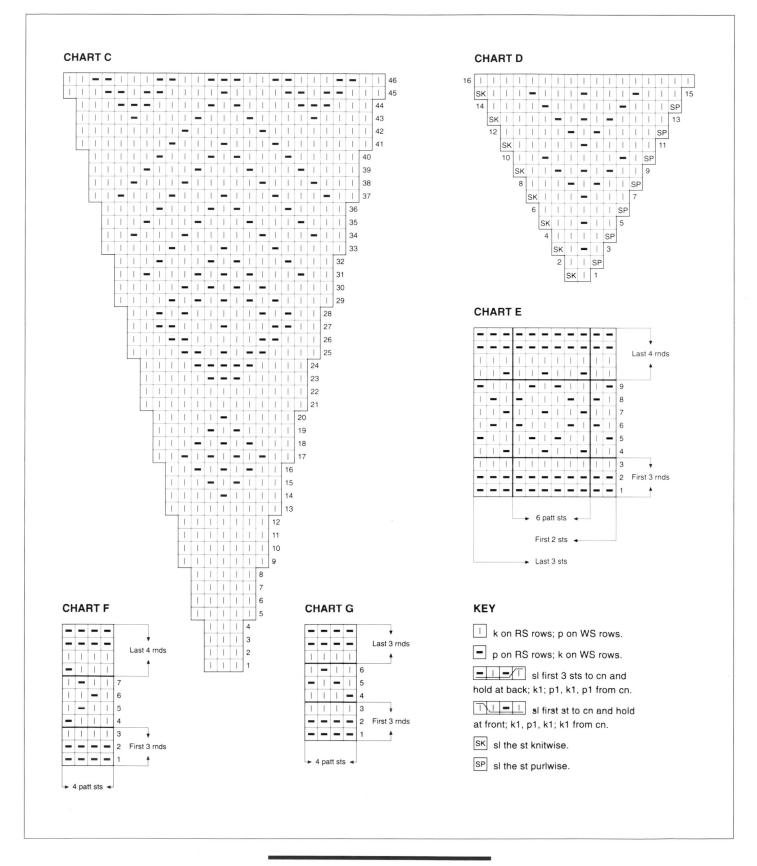

CHART C

CHART D

CHART E

CHART F

CHART G

KEY

| | k on RS rows; p on WS rows.

| — | p on RS rows; k on WS rows.

sl first 3 sts to cn and hold at back; k1; p1, k1, p1 from cn.

sl first 3t to cn and hold at front; k1, p1, k1; k1 from cn.

SK sl the st knitwise.

SP sl the st purlwise.

RH needle; turn.

Cont in this manner from row 3 of chart D, until row 16 of chart D has been completed and all shoulder sts have been incoporated into gusset.

Place 17 gusset sts on a holder.★★

Right Neck Gusset

Place right front and right back shoulder sts on 2 separate double-pointed 2¼mm (US 1) needles. With 2¾mm (US 2) needle, holding WS of right front and back shoulders tog and beg at armhole edge of shoulder, cast off shoulder sts tog until 8 sts rem on each of front and back shoulder needles at neck edge.

Complete as left neck gusset from ★★ to ★★, but reading 'front shoulder' for 'back shoulder' and vice versa.

SLEEVES

With RS facing and 2¾mm (US 2) needles, work rnd 46 of gusset chart C across 25 sts of gusset; pick up and k 149 sts evenly around armhole edge to complete rnd. 174 sts.

Place a st marker on RH needle to mark beg of rnd and working in rnds, set patt as follows—

Next rnd: Turn gusset chart C upside down and work chart rnd 45 across 25 gusset sts; work first 2 sts of rnd 1 of chart E as indicated; rep 6 patt sts of chart E 24 times; work last 3 sts of chart E as indicated.

Shape Gusset

Beg shaping gussets as follows—

Next rnd: Ssk; keeping continuity, work rnd 44 of chart C across centre 21 gusset sts; k2tog; work rnd 2 of chart E as set over 149 sleeve sts.

Cont as set, work rnd 3 of chart E and then rep rnds 4 through 9 of chart 7 times, AND AT THE SAME TIME work rnds 43 through 1 of gusset chart C, dec 1 st at each side of gusset on every foll 4th rnd as indicated until 3 gusset sts rem. 152 **sts.**

Next rnd: Sl 1-k2tog-psso; work first of last 4 rnds of chart E as set over 149 sleeve sts.

Next rnd: P1 (seam st); k to end of rnd. P 2 rnds.

Shape Lower Sleeve

Next rnd: P1 (seam st); k2tog; k to last 2 sts; ssk. 148 sts.

Cont to p seam st to cuff, dec 1 st at each side of seam st on every foll 4th rnd until 124 sts rem, then on every foll 3rd rnd until 68 sts rem, AND AT THE SAME TIME work remainder of sleeve in patt bands as follows—

Work 28 rnds in st st.

Working chart F, work first 3 rnds once, then rep rnds 4 through 7 of chart 9 times, then work last 4 rnds of chart, thus working 43 chart F rnds in total.

Work 25 rnds in st st.

Working chart G, work first 3 rnds once,

I adapted a chart from my pattern library for the shell motif on Cape Cod and arranged it in panels between lightly textured wishbone cables. On the sleeves, I have worked bands of tiny textured patterns, highlighted on a smooth stocking-stitch background. I love the idea of subtle, barely discernable design elements, and so I patterned the underarm and neck gussets.

*T*he style of Cape Cod is
elegant and understated.
*Knitted in a luxurious fine blend of
silk and wool, this design is
reminiscent of grains of sand blowing
across a beach. (For a full description
of the yarn used see page 127)*

then rep rnds 4 through 6 of chart 10
times, then work last 3 rnds of chart, thus
working 36 chart F rnds in total.
68 sts rem.
Work 25 rnds in st st without shaping.
Working chart A and rep 4 patt sts 17
times in each rnd, work first 3 rnds once,
then rep rnds 4 through 7 of chart 3
times, then work last 3 rnds of chart, thus
working 18 chart A rnds in total.
Cast off knitwise.

NECKBAND

With RS facing and 2¼mm (US 1)
needles, beg at back neck st holder and
pick up sts as follows—
(K12; k2tog; k4; k2tog; k27; k2tog; k4;
k2tog; k12) all from back neck holder;
there are now 63 sts on needle; k 17 sts
from left neck gusset holder; pick up and
k 21 sts evenly down left side of front
neck to front neck holder; (k1; k2tog; k4;
k2tog; k27; k2tog; k4; k2tog; k1) all from
front neck holder; there are now 142 sts on
needle; pick up and k 21 sts evenly up right
side of front neck; k 17 sts from right neck
gusset holder to complete rnd. 180 sts.
Place a st marker on RH needle to mark
beg of rnd and working chart A in rnds
and rep 4 patt sts 45 times in each rnd,
work first 3 rnds once, rep rnds 4 through
7 of chart twice, then work last 3 rnds
of chart, thus working 14 chart A rnds
in total.
Cast off knitwise.

FINISHING

Darn in loose ends. Rinse, short spin and
dry garment to size on a woolly board (see
page 124). Do not press.

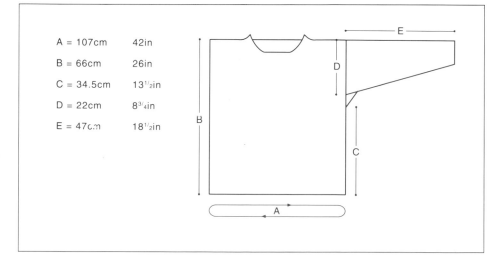

A = 107cm	42in
B = 66cm	26in
C = 34.5cm	13½in
D = 22cm	8¾in
E = 47cm	18½in

NOVA SCOTIA

RATING ★ ★ ★ ★

SIZES
To fit small [medium, large]
*Directions for larger sizes are given in brackets.
Where there is only one set of figures, it applies
to all sizes.*

KNITTED
MEASUREMENTS
Underarm, excluding gussets
110[116.5,123]cm (44[46½,49¼]in)
Length 63[65,67]cm (24¾[25½,26½]in)
Sleeve length 46[47,48]cm (18[18½,19]in)

MATERIALS
Yarn weight used: 4-ply silk and wool
(US sport)
31[33,34] x 20g (¾oz) balls of Rowan *Silk
and Wool* in shade no. 860 'Pine'
1 set of double-pointed *or* circular 2¼mm
(US 1) and 2¾mm (US 2) needles
1 cable needle
8 stitch holders
Stitch markers

TENSION (GAUGE)
34 sts and 45 rows to 10cm (4in)
measured over chart A patt, using 2¾mm
(US 2) needles

BODY
Body is worked in one piece to armhole.
With 2¼mm (US 1) needles, cast on
340[360,380] sts.
Place a st marker on RH needle to mark
beg of rnd, then making sure cast-on edge
is not twisted and working in rnds (RS
always facing), work k1b (k1 through
back loop), p1 rib for 7cm (2¾in), slipping
marker on each rnd.
Inc rnd: *M1, k10; rep from * to end of
rnd. 374[396,418] sts.
Change to 2¾mm (US 2) needles and
reading chart from right to left, set chart A
patt as follows—
Chart A rnd 1. Rep 11 patt sts of rnd 1
of chart A 34[36,38] times.
Reading every chart rnd from right to
left, cont in chart A patt as set, rep 10 patt
rnds until body measures 32.5[34,35.5]cm
(12¾[13¼,14]in) from beg, slipping marker

*T*his design is a new look at an
old Scottish theme. For me, the
true romance of the Scottish gansey
tradition is centred on the fact that
women made ganseys for those they
loved and often reserved the finest for
the one they loved the most. My aim
in designing Nova Scotia is to
celebrate that idea by creating a
gansey to be knitted for a lover.

on every rnd throughout.
Dec rnd: *K2tog, k9; rep from * to end
of rnd. 340[360,380] sts.
Begin Gussets and Border Pattern
Beg gussets and set chart B border patt as
follows—
Chart B rnd 1: Keeping marker in place
to mark first st for beg of rnd and beg of
first underarm gusset, *m1; k1; m1; work
first 0[2,1] sts of rnd 1 of chart B as
indicated; rep 6 patt sts 28[29,31] times;
work last 1[3,2] sts of chart as indicated*;

place a st marker on RH needle to mark
next st for beg of 2nd underarm gusset,
then rep from * to * once more. (The k st
and the inc sts form the gussets – there are
now 3 sts in each gusset.)
Cont to work chart B patt as set over
169[179,189] sts of front and back, and
working all gusset sts in st st, inc 1 st at
each side of each gusset on every foll 4th
rnd until there are 19 sts in each gusset
and all 33 rnds of chart B have been
completed. 376[396,416] sts.
Divide for Yokes
Place first 19 sts of rnd (gusset) on a
holder, leave next 169[179,189] sts (front
yoke sts) on a spare needle, place next 19
sts (gusset) on a holder. 169[179,189] sts
of back yoke rem.
Back Yoke
Beg with a WS row and working back
and forth in rows, inc evenly across
169[179,189] sts of back yoke on next
row as follows—
★★Inc row (WS): P71[76,81]; (m1, p2)
twice; m1; p1; k17; p1; (m1, p2) twice;
m1; p71[76,81]. 175[185,195] sts.
Reading charts from right to left for RS
(odd-numbered) rows and from left to
right for WS (even-numbered) rows and
beg all charts from row 1, set yoke patt as
follows—
Chart row 1 (RS): Work chart C over
first 68[73,78] sts, working first 4[0,5] sts
of chart as indicated, rep 9 patt sts 7[8,8]
times and working last st of chart as
indicated; work chart E over next 13 sts;
work chart F over next 13 sts; work chart
E over next 13 sts; work chart D over last
68[73,78] sts, working first st of chart as
indicated, rep 9 patt sts 7[8,8] times and
working last 4[0,5] sts of chart as
indicated.★★
Cont in patts as set, rep all rows of each
chart until chart F has been worked 4
times in all, thus working 104 chart F
rows in total.
Cont in patt as set, but working 13 centre
sts in rev st st, until back yoke measures
22[22.5,23]cm (8½[8¾,9]in) from top of
gussets, ending with RS facing for next
row.
Dec for shoulders as follows—

*T*he main motif on Nova Scotia is a heart, worked in moss stitch and outlined in cabled stitches. The other patterns all have connections with the sea. Instead of the traditional method of working the shoulder straps from neck to sleeve, I have designed them so that the cables can continue, like those of the front and back, and run through the neckband. This is my finest traditionally-styled gansey and is worked in a beautiful silk and wool blend. It is a garment to knit and wear with pride.

Dec row (RS): K3; (k2tog, k1) 16[17, 18] times; k2tog; k2; place these last 38[40, 42] sts on a holder; keeping continuity, work next 65[69,73] sts in patt and place these sts on a separate holder; k2; k2tog; (k1, k2tog) 16[17,18] times; k3; place these last 38[40,42] sts on a separate holder.

Front Yoke
With WS facing, rejoin yarn to 169[179, 189] sts of front yoke and working back and forth in rows, work as back from ** to **.

Cont in patts as set, rep all rows of each chart until chart F has been worked 3 times in all, thus working 78 chart F rows in total and ending with RS facing for next row.

Shape Front Neck
Next row (RS): Keeping continuity, work 70[75,80] sts in patt; place next 35 sts on a holder for front neck; turn, leaving rem sts on a spare needle. Keeping continuity of patt throughout, shape left side of neck as follows—
***Dec 1 st at neck edge on every foll row 6[6,8] times, then at same edge on every foll alt row 9[11,11] times. 55[58,61] sts rem.
Work without shaping until there are same number of rows as back to shoulder, ending with RS facing for next row.***
Dec for shoulder as follows—
Dec row (RS): K3; (k2tog, k1) 16[17, 18] times; k2tog; k2.
Place rem 38[40,42] sts on a holder.
With RS facing, rejoin yarn to right side of neck and keeping continuity, shape as left side of neck from *** to ***.
Dec for shoulder as follows—
Dec row (RS): K2; k2tog; (k1, k2tog) 16[17,18] times; k3.
Place rem 38[40,42] sts on a holder.

RIGHT SHOULDER STRAP

Place right front and right back shoulder sts on 2 separate double-pointed needles or on 1 circular 2¾mm (US 2) needle. (**Note:** For circular needle, place the sts so that both the pointed ends are at the armhole edge.)
With WS facing and a contrasting yarn, using 'thumb method', cast on 13 sts onto armhole end of needle holding right back shoulder sts, then turn.
Foundation row 1 (RS): With armhole end of needle holding right front shoulder sts and using contrasting yarn, k across 13 cast-on sts; turn.
Foundation row 2: With needle holding back shoulder sts and using contrasting yarn, p across the 13 sts; turn.
Break off contrasting yarn.
Join in main yarn and beg with row 1 of chart E, set chart patt on next row as follows—
Chart E row 1 (RS): Work first 12 sts of row 1 of chart E across first 12 sts of strap; then p tog last st of strap with first st from back shoulder; turn.
Chart E row 2: Work first 12 sts of row 2 of chart E across first 12 sts of strap; ssk last st of strap tog with first st from front shoulder; turn.
Cont in this manner, rep 8 patt rows of chart E until all shoulder sts have been incorporated into shoulder strap.
Break off yarn and place 13 strap sts on a holder.**

LEFT SHOULDER STRAP

Place left front and left back shoulder sts on needles as for right shoulder strap.
With WS facing and a contrasting yarn, using 'thumb method', cast on 13 sts onto armhole end of needle holding left front shoulder sts, then turn.
Work as right shoulder strap from ** to **, but reading 'back shoulder' for 'front shoulder' and vice versa.

SLEEVES
Remove contrasting yarn from shoulder straps and place 13 loops formed by first row of main yarn on 2 holders.
With RS facing and 2¾mm (US 2) needles, k 19 sts from gusset holder; pick up and k 74[76,78] sts evenly up armhole edge to shoulder strap; work sts from shoulder strap as follows—
K2; k2tog; k1; k2tog; k1; k2tog; k3; pick up and k 74[76,78] sts evenly down armhole edge to complete rnd. 177[181,185] sts.

Shape Gusset
Place a st marker on RH needle to mark beg of rnd and working in rnds, beg shaping gusset and set chart B patt as follows—
Chart B rnd 1: Ssk; k15; k2tog; rep 6 patt sts of rnd 1 of chart B 26[27,27] times; work first 2[0,4] sts of patt rep over last 2[0,4] sts of sleeve.
Cont in chart B patt as set over sleeve sts until chart row 29 has been completed,

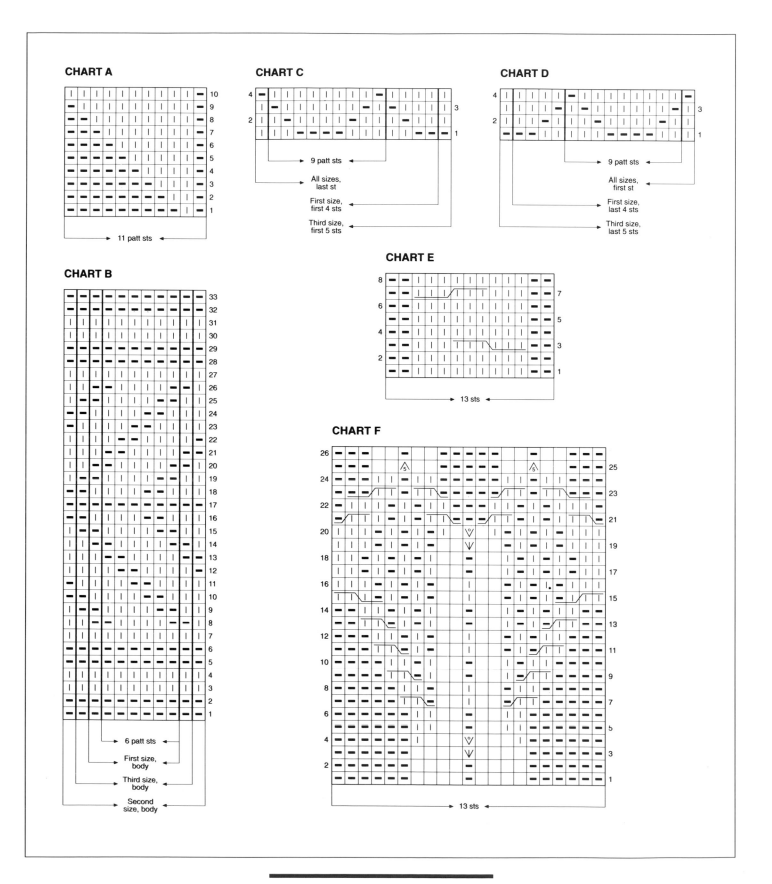

AND AT THE SAME TIME working gusset sts in st st throughout, shape gussets by dec 1 st at each side of gusset on every foll 4th rnd until 3 gusset sts in st st rem. 161[165,169] sts.

Work 3 rnds in patt B as set without shaping.

Chart B rnd 33: Sl 1-p2tog-psso; work in chart B patt to end of rnd.

Inc on next rnd as follows—

Next rnd: P1 (seam st); k1[3,5]; *m1, k12; rep from * to last 1[3,5] sts; m1;

KEY

☐ k on RS rows; p on WS rows.

☐ p on RS rows; k on WS rows.

☐ no stitch.

Ⓥ (k1b, k1) into same st, then insert left hand needle point between the vertical strand that runs down between the 2 sts just made and k into this strand, making the third st of the group.

Ⓥ (p1, yo, p1) into same st, making 3 sts in the group.

▭ sl first st to cn and hold at back; k2; p1 from cn.

▭ sl first 2 sts to cn and hold at front; p1; k2 from cn.

▭ sl first 2 sts to cn and hold at back; k2; k1, p1 from cn.

▭ sl first 2 sts to cn and hold at front; p1, k1; k2 from cn.

▭ sl first 2 sts to cn and hold at front; p2; k2 from cn.

▭ sl first 2 sts to cn and hold at back; k2; p2 from cn.

▭ sl decrease 5 sts tog thus – sl 3 knitwise, one at a time, with yarn at back, drop yarn, then * pass the second st on right hand needle over the first (centre) st; sl the centre st back to left hand needle and pass the next st on left hand needle over it **; sl the centre st back to right hand needle and rep from * to ** once more; p the centre st.

▭ sl first 3 sts to cn and hold at front; k3; k3 from cn.

▭ sl first 3 sts to cn and hold at back; k3; k3 from cn.

k1[3,5]. 173[177,181] sts.

Set chart A patt on next rnd as follows—

Chart A rnd 1: P1 (seam st); work last 3[0,2] sts of rnd 1 of chart A; rep 11 patt sts 15[16,16] times; work first 4[0,2] sts of chart.

Cont to p seam st, work 1 rnd in patt as set without shaping.

Shape Lower Sleeve

Next rnd: P1; k2tog; keeping continuity, work in patt to last 2 sts; ssk.

Cont to p seam st to cuff and keeping continuity of patt, dec 1 st at each side of seam st on every foll 4th rnd until 117[121,125] sts rem, then on every foll 3rd rnd until 91[95,99] sts rem.

Cuff

Dec rnd: K3[0,2]; *k2tog, k3; rep from * to last 3[0,2] sts; k3[0,2]. 74[76,80] sts.

Change to 2¼mm (US 1) and work k1b, p1 rib until sleeve measures 46[47,48]cm (18[18½,19]in).

Cast off in rib.

NECKBAND

With RS facing and 2¼mm (US 1) needles, beg at back neck st holder and keeping continuity of cable patts, pick up sts as follows—

From back neck holder — (k1b, p1) 6[7,8] times; k1b; work chart E over next 13 sts; (k1b, p1) 6 times; k1b; work chart E over next 13 sts; (k1b, p1) 6[7,8] times; k1b; from left shoulder strap holder — work chart E over 13 sts of strap; pick up

and k 21[23,25] sts evenly down left side of front neck to front neck holder; from front neck holder — work chart E over first 11 sts; (k1b, p1) 6 times; k1b; work chart E over next 11 sts; pick up and k 21[23,25] sts evenly up right side of neck to shoulder strap holder; from right shoulder strap holder — work chart E over 13 sts of strap to complete rnd. 168[176,184] sts.

Place a st marker on RH needle to mark beg of rnd and working in rnds, work next rnd as follows—

Next rnd: Work in patt as set over sts of back neck and left shoulder strap; across sts picked up along left side of neck work — (k1b, p1) 9[10,11] times; k1b; p2; work in patt as set over sts of centre front neck; across sts picked up along right side of neck work — p2; (k1b, p1) 9[10,11] times; k1b; work in patt as set over sts of right shoulder strap.

Cont working chart E patt and rib as set until neckband measures 5cm (2in).

Next rnd: Work all rib sts in rib as set and dec 4 sts across each of six 13-st cable by working — p2; k2tog; k1; sl 1-k2tog-psso; k1; k2tog; p2. 144[152,160] sts.

Work 6 rnds in st st.

Cast off loosely and evenly knitwise.

FINISHING

Darn in loose ends. Rinse, short spin and dry garment to size on a woolly board (see page 124). Do not press.

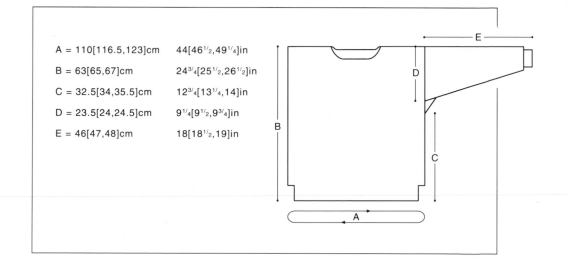

A = 110[116.5,123]cm   44[46½,49¼]in

B = 63[65,67]cm   24¾[25½,26½]in

C = 32.5[34,35.5]cm   12¾[13¼,14]in

D = 23.5[24,24.5]cm   9¼[9½,9¾]in

E = 46[47,48]cm   18[18½,19]in

KNITTING TECHNIQUES

This chapter provides instructions and illustrations for the knitting techniques used in this book. It also gives an overview of the method of working traditional circular fisher ganseys and Fair Isle type sweaters. Circular knitting, neck and underarm gussets, shoulder straps and steeks are all outlined here in order to give a general understanding of these particular techniques.

However, please note that the pattern for each individual sweater gives detailed and exact instructions for working any particular feature used in the design. If you are a newcomer to any of these techniques, it is important that you read the information given here and then read through the pattern before you start knitting, so that you will have a clear understanding of the work.

SIZES

Most of the patterns in this book are written in a range of sizes. Instructions for the first size are given outside a set of brackets [ ], with the larger sizes following on in order within the brackets.

Look at the actual measurements when choosing which size to make. Some garments have a generous amount of 'ease', so you may prefer to knit a smaller size than normal if the finished result is too large for your taste. Once you have decided on a size, mark the relevant figures throughout the pattern to avoid confusion.

YARNS

A specific brand and shade of yarn is quoted for each design in the book. To avoid the frus-tration of being unable to obtain specific yarns, a detailed description of each yarn used is given on page 127. The yarn description should be used as a guide if you are looking for a generic equivalent. But remember only to substitute a different yarn after first making a test swatch and checking that it matches the required tension (gauge).

Changing yarns could mean that you will need more or less yarn than stated in the pattern, even though both yarns may be packaged in the same weight balls. Each type of yarn has a different number of metres (yards) per ball. There-fore, before purchasing a sub-stitute yarn, you will need to determine how many metres (yards) are required. The num-ber of metres (yards) per ball is given in the yarn descriptions on page 127.

TENSION (GAUGE)

The tension (gauge) quoted in a pattern has been achieved by the designer of the garment who uses it to make all the stitch and row calculations. As your tension is personal to you, you *must* knit a tension (gauge) swatch before starting work to ensure that the finished sweater is the intended size.

Using the specified yarn and needles, and working in the appropriate stitch or pattern, knit a swatch about 15cm (6in) square. (To make a Fair Isle swatch, see page 123.) Place the finished swatch on a padded surface, gently smooth it into shape, then secure the edges with pins placed at right angles to the fabric.

Using pins as markers at each end, measure out 10cm (4in) horizontally across the centre of the swatch for the stitch tension (gauge) and vertically down the swatch for the row tension (gauge). Fewer stitches than stated means that your work is too loose and you need to try again with smaller needles; more stitches than stated indicates that you should try again with larger needles. Changing the needle size is not important as long as you obtain the correct tension.

A CIRCULAR GANSEY

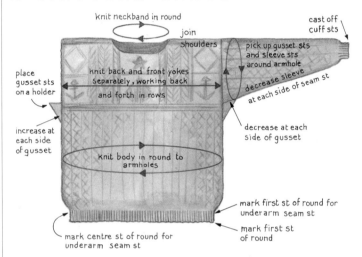

The illustration above shows the circular method of knitting applied to a traditional fisher gansey shape. To begin, the body stitches are cast on, onto either a set of double-pointed knitting needles or onto a sin-gle circular knitting needle. This is so that the body can be worked in the round (with the right side always facing) to the armholes. (See page 118 for cast-on techniques.)

Before the knitting is begun, the first stitch of the round is marked to indicate the start of each new round.

Seam Stitches

The body ribbing is worked until it is the required depth. Then the first and centre stitch of the round are each marked (and sometimes worked in a different stitch) in order to indicate each underarm stitch. These underarm stitches are known as 'seam stitches', and they divide the round into *front* and *back* stitches.

Underarm Gussets

The body is worked in the round without shaping until about 8 or 10cm (3 or 4in) below the armholes, when the diamond-shaped underarm gussets are begun (below).

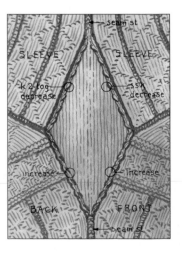

117

These gussets are an integral part of a traditional circular fisher gansey and are very much easier to work than they may appear. They are started by increasing one stitch at each side of each seam stitch, thus giving three stitches in each gusset. The gussets are then increased regularly to the required width at the armhole.

Front and Back Yokes
When the armholes are reached, the gusset stitches are placed on holders, and the front and back yokes are worked separately, back and forth in rows. The body is joined at the shoulders by either casting off the stitches together or working shoulder straps (see page 121).

Circular Sleeves
The sleeves are also worked in the round and are begun by knitting the gusset stitches from the holders and picking up stitches around the arm-holes to form a round. As the sleeve progresses, the under-arm gusset is decreased gradually until only the centre seam stitch remains.

This seam stitch is then marked as the first stitch of the round, and then the sleeve itself is decreased regularly at each side of the seam stitch. The decreases at each side of the gusset and sleeve seam stitch are worked to give a symmetrical appearance. 'Slip, knit' (ssk) is the decrease that slants to the left, while 'knit 2 together' (k2tog) slants to the right.

When the sleeve is the required width above the cuff, a decrease round is worked, the cuff is ribbed and the stitches cast off.

Neckband
Lastly, the neckband stitches are picked up and the neck-band is worked in the round to complete the garment.

CASTING ON TECHNIQUES FOR GANSEYS

There are a number of meth-ods of casting on which are used in the making of tradi-tional circular ganseys. Though they differ both in execution and appearance, they have one main purpose in common, and that is to pro-duce a strong and flexible edge. This was obviously a very important feature of a garment which was intended for hard wear.

For the designs in this book you may use any type of cast-on you prefer, but if you intend the garment for rugged use, or if you simply wish to include all the authentic details in your sweater, I would rec-ommend using one of the methods shown here. All cast-on methods can be worked on either straight double-pointed needles or a circular needle.

Cable Edge Cast-on
The cable edge cast-on is an attractive and practical cast-on. You will find that you can use it on almost any type of garment. One great advantage of this method is that you do not have to judge any lengths of yarn in advance, as the entire edge is worked from a single strand, straight from the ball of yarn. The only restric-tion is that you must knit or purl into the front of all the stitches on the first round worked, otherwise the stitches will untwist from the cast-on position.

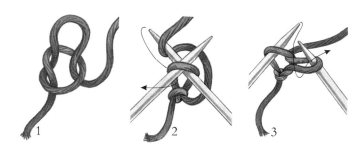 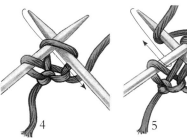

Make a starting or 'slip' loop (step 1 above) and place it on the left-hand needle. Insert the right-hand needle, from front to back, through the starting loop. Wrap the yarn around the right-hand needle and pull a loop through (step 2). Place this loop on the left-hand needle, turning it (see arrow in step 3) so that it lies in the correct position and withdraw the right-hand needle (step 4). There are now two stitches on the left-hand needle. *Insert the right-hand needle between the two stitches, wrap the yarn around the needle and pull a loop through (step 5). Place this loop on the left-hand nee-dle as before and withdraw the right-hand needle (step 6). Repeat from * until you have cast on the required number of stitches.

Two-Colour Cable Edge Cast-on
The two-colour cable edge cast-on is the same cast-on as described above, except that the stitches are cast on in two alternating colours. If you are not familiar with the cable edge cast-on, I would suggest that you first practise a few stitches with one colour, before trying it with two colours. I have used this cast-on in my design *Norway* (page 76), and the result is very dec-orative as well as practical.

With the first colour, make a starting loop as for the single colour cable edge cast-on. Insert the the right-hand needle, from front to back, through the starting loop; wrap the second colour around the right-hand needle and pull a loop through (step 1). Place this loop on the left-hand needle as for the single colour cable edge (see arrow in step 3) and withdraw the right-hand needle. There are now two stitches on the left-

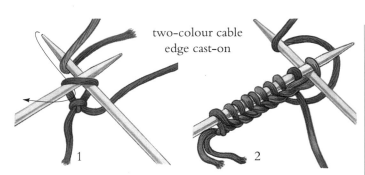

two-colour cable
edge cast-on

1

2

hand needle. Proceed as for the single colour cable edge, but picking up alternating colours from the back of the left-hand needle (step 2).

Do not work the first row of ribbing in the round, but work from the last stitch cast on, back to the first stitch cast on. This is so that the side facing you while casting on will appear on the right side of the circular garment. After this first row, join the edge into a circle and proceed in the round.

Double Yarn Cast-on
The double yarn cast-on is a very basic method of producing a strong edge for tough wear. It is featured in the child's design *Fife* (page 29).

Measure a length of yarn, roughly six times as long as the edge to be cast on. Make a starting loop at the centre of this length of yarn, and place it

on the needle. These long ends form the doubled yarn. Holding the single yarn (from the ball) in the right hand and the doubled yarn over the thumb of the left, loop the doubled yarn over the needle, and then wrap the single yarn over needle from right and draw through a stitch (below left). Pull the doubled yarn gently to fasten the stitch. Continue in this manner until the required number of stitches have been cast on.

Knotted Edge Cast-on
Working the knotted edge cast-on is such a slow process, that I recommend it only if you need a very tough edge.

Make a starting loop, leaving a long loose end which is roughly three times as long as the edge to be cast on. Place the loop on the needle. Using the double cast-on thumb method, cast on one stitch as shown (step 1). There are now two stitches on the needle. Then, using the tip of the left-hand needle, lift the first stitch on the right-hand needle over the second, thus casting it off (step 2) and leaving one stitch on the right-hand needle. *Cast on two more stitches using the double cast-on thumb method, then cast off the first of these two over the second. Repeat from * until the required number of stitches have been cast on.

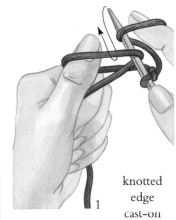

knotted
edge
cast-on

1

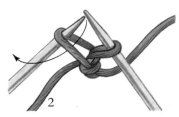

2

Channel Islands Cast-On
The Channel Islands cast-on is very attractive and practical. It works best with a k1, p1 rib where the knotted stitch is worked as a knit stitch and the yarn over is worked as a purl stitch. I have used this edge on both the *Eriskay* and *Nova Scotia* designs (pages 16 and 111).

Cut two strands of yarn roughly three times as long as

the edge to be cast on. Wrap the doubled strands around the left thumb twice, and insert the right-hand needle, from below, under all four strands on the left thumb (step 1 below). With a single end of the yarn from the ball, draw a loop through the loops on the thumb to make the first stitch on the right-hand needle. This first step is a little awkward. The trick is to hang on to all the yarn ends until you have secured the stitch.

*Take the single yarn to the front and over the needle to make the next stitch (a yarn over) as shown (see step 2 below), then wrap the yarn around the left thumb twice and insert the needle from below under all four strands on the thumb; with the single yarn, knit the next stitch. Repeat from * until the required number of stitches are cast on. For an even number of stitches, the last stitch cast on will be a yarn over, therefore do not forget to include it when joining up the stitches into a round.

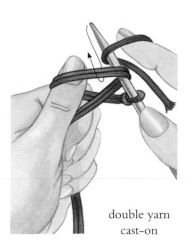

double yarn
cast-on

Channel Islands
cast-on

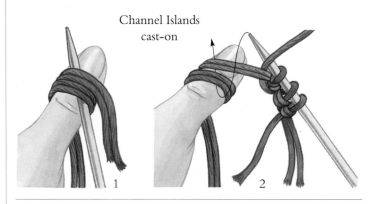

1

2

CIRCULAR KNITTING CAST-ON

All circular knitted garments must be worked with either a set of double-pointed needles or a circular needle. The

choice of which type to use is a matter of personal preference, as the knitted results will be the same.

Circular Needles

Circular needles are a relatively modern invention and are undoubtedly easier to handle than double-pointed needles. For this reason I would recommend them to the newcomer. Circular needles are produced in a variety of lengths, as it is vital that there are a sufficient number of stitches to fit around the needle, for any given project. The needle does not need to be the same length as the circumference of the knitting; indeed, the needle can be considerably shorter, but it must not be longer. For example, the body of an adult gansey will require a 60 to 80cm (24 to 32in) circular needle, whereas the upper sleeve and neckband, which have a much shorter circumference, will need to be worked on a 40cm (16in) length.

The lower sleeves and cuffs are usually too narrow to be worked on a circular needle, in which case, it is necessary to transfer to double-pointed needles when the circle becomes too small. I would recommend using 20cm (8in) double-pointed knitting needles for areas with a small circumference.

Casting on with a Circular Needle

To begin your work on a circular needle, cast on the total number of stitches using your preferred method. If only one needle is required for your chosen cast-on, then use either end of the needle. If the method requires two needles, then use both ends of the needle. The illustration (above) shows the stitches cast on with the cable edge method. To

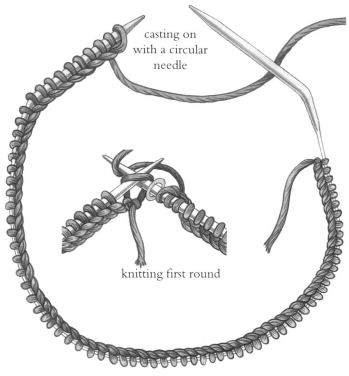

casting on with a circular needle

knitting first round

join the stitches into a circle or round, first turn the work so that the last stitch cast on is at the tip of the right-hand needle. Then making sure that the cast on edge is not twisted, knit into the first stitch to begin the round (see above).

Double-pointed Needles

Double-pointed needles are generally available in sets of four, although some European manufacturers make sets of five. Traditionally, British fisher ganseys were made on

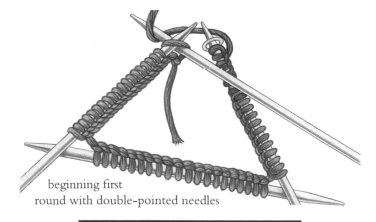

beginning first round with double-pointed needles

four 12 or 14in (30 or 35cm) needles, using a fifth needle if the garment was especially wide. The entire garment would be worked on the longer needles, although now many knitters find it easier to transfer to shorter needles for lower sleeves and cuffs.

Casting On with Double-pointed Needles

To begin your work on a set of four double-pointed needles, cast on the total number of stitches required and distrib-

ute them as evenly as possible over three of the needles. Making sure that the edge is not twisted, draw up the last stitch on the third needle so that it meets the first stitch on the first needle, forming a triangle. Then, using the fourth needle, join the stitches into a round or circle by knitting into first stitch (see below), and continue to work to the end of the first needle. This needle is then free to work the stitches on the next needle, and so on. If you find, when knitting, that the tension between the last stitch on one needle and the first stitch on the next is too loose, compensate by working the first stitch on each needle with a little more tension, and move one or two stitches on each round to the adjacent needle to vary the change-over points from round to round.

SHOULDER VARIATIONS

There are a number of beautiful and effective traditional ways of adding detail to the shoulder of the fisher gansey. Some are very simple and none are difficult, though the results are invariably sophisticated.

Casting Off Stitches Together

Casting off front and back shoulder stitches together is the easiest possible way to join shoulder seams. This can be worked on the right side as I have done in *Cornwall* (page 36), to produce a raised ridge, or on the wrong side as in *Filey* (page 49), for a very unobtrusive finish.

Hold the needles with the front and back shoulder

stitches parallel to each other in the left hand (with wrong sides together to work on the right side, or right sides together to work on the wrong side). Insert the right-hand needle through the first stitch on each needle and knit these stitches together. Then insert the needle through the next stitch on each needle and knit these stitches together. Cast off the first stitch on the right needle, over the second. Continue in this manner until all stitches have been cast off (see below).

When working with heavier yarns, it is usually necessary to use a larger size for the right-hand needle, because the cast-off edge will tend to be too tight otherwise. If you find this is so even with a finer yarn, then always use a size larger needle to cast off.

Neck Gussets

Neck gussets are a very clever way of adding shaping at the point where the shoulder curves into the neck (below).

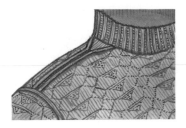

The traditional neck gusset is featured in *Norfolk* (page 40), and I have added a textured pattern to it in *Cape Cod* (page 105).

The shoulder stitches are cast off together, from the armhole edge towards the neck, until the desired number of stitches remain on each needle, plus the stitch on the cast-off needle. The triangular neck gusset is then begun by knitting the first stitch from one shoulder needle, thus having the cast-off stitch and the stitch just knitted on the right-hand needle. The work is then turned and the two stitches are worked on the wrong side, then the first stitch from the other shoulder needle is worked (thereby increasing the neck gusset to three stitches). Each consecutive row is worked by turning and working across the gusset stitches and picking up a stitch from a shoulder needle, until all the shoulder stitches are incorporated into the gusset. The stitches are then placed on a holder and picked up and worked to form part of the neckband.

Shoulder Straps

There are two basic types of shoulder straps, both of which have been most extensively used in the traditional ganseys from Scotland. The first, which I have used in *Lochinver* (page 24), is worked as a continuation of the front yoke, so that the shoulder pattern is worked entirely in one piece. This means that the 'shoulder' seam is positioned at the back edge of the patterned strap, and not at the centre of the shoulder, as is usual. The back yoke is shortened to compensate, and the shoulder strap and

back shoulder stitches are grafted together to avoid a visible seamline (top above).

The more dramatic shoulder strap is worked at right angles to the shoulders (above). I have used it in traditional fashion on *Stornoway*, *Eriskay* and *Fife*, and in a less traditional way on *Nova Scotia*. To work this type of strap, the shoulder stitches are placed on needles, and the stitches required for the strap are cast on with a contrasting waste yarn, at the neck edge of one of the shoulder needles. A row is worked in waste yarn, then the main yarn is joined in and the chosen pattern is worked across the shoulder-strap stitches, with the last stitch of the strap being knitted together with the first stitch from the first shoulder needle. The work is then turned, and the next row of pattern is worked across the strap, with the last stitch of the

strap being knitted together with the first stitch from the second shoulder needle. Each consecutive row is worked by turning the work and knitting together the last stitch of the strap with the next stitch from the shoulder needle. Thus the strap stitches remain constant, and the shoulder stitches are decreased into the strap one at a time, at the end of every row. When all the shoulder stitches are used up the strap will be completed to the armhole edge.

The strap stitches are then placed on holders and are picked up with the armhole stitches when the sleeve is begun. The strap pattern can then continue down the sleeve. The waste yarn is later removed and the loops formed by the first row of the strap are worked as part of the neckband.

Grafting

Grafting, also called Kitchener stitch, is the method used to join stitches together in order to avoid a seamline. In this book, I have used the method on the shoulder strap of *Lochinver* (page 24), and on the shoulders of *Norway* (page 76) and *Faroe* (page 81).

Thread a darning needle with the main yarn, roughly three times the length of the shoulder seam. Graft stitches together as shown (below),

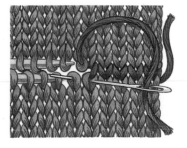

gently pulling the thread as you go along, until the new set of loops formed are equal in size to those of the knitting. Darn in both yarn ends on completion.

READING CHARTS

Most of the textured and coloured patterns in this book are worked from charts. The symbol in each square represents one stitch or action, which is explained in the accompanying key. Each row of squares represents one row or round of knitting. All charts are read from the first row or round at the bottom, to the last row or round, at the top.

On designs which are worked in flat pieces, *the odd-numbered rows are right side rows and are worked from right to left, and even-numbered rows are wrong side rows and are worked from left to right.*

On textured circular ganseys, each round is worked with the right side facing the knitter and all rounds are read from the right. The back and front yokes are worked back and forth in rows, and therefore at this point, the charts are read as for flat pieces above from * to *. Charts which are used for both the circular and flat parts of the garment are therefore numbered on every row or round on the right side of the chart, and on even-numbered rows on the left side.

The two Fair Isle type designs in the book are worked entirely in the round and therefore each round of the charts are read from right to left.

CIRCULAR FAIR ISLE

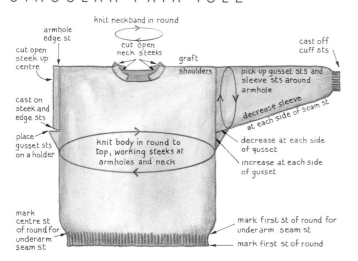

The circular Fair Isle knitting method is well worth becoming acquainted with, as it is the fastest and easiest way of knitting colour patterns. *Norway* (page 76) and *Faroe* (page 81) are both knit in this way.

The illustration (above) shows the circular method of knitting a Fair Isle sweater. The entire garment is worked in the round. This means that the colour pattern will always be facing, so that you can see the pattern at all times. It also means that the colour pattern

is worked using only knit stitches, as there is no need to turn the work and purl the wrong side.

The sweater is worked to the armholes in the same way as the traditional fisher gansey. The armhole gusset stitches are placed on holders and extra stitches (called steek stitches — see below) are cast on immediately above the gusset holders so that the front and back yokes can be worked in the round.

The neck is worked by placing the centre stitches of the front neck (and later, back neck) on a holder and immediately casting on steek stitches so that the shoulders can be worked in the round. The neck is shaped by decreasing stitches at each side of the steek.

All the steek stitches are cast off on the last round of knitting. Then the shoulder stitches are grafted together. The sleeves and gussets are worked as described for the fisher gansey. The neck steeks are cut open up the centre and the neckband stitches are picked up and worked in the round. The steeks are then trimmed and stitched in position.

STRANDED KNITTING

In Fair Isle knitting, a maximum of two colours are used in any one round, with the colour not in immediate use being stranded across the back of the work. It is important to strand the yarn evenly across the back; strands which are too loose will produce uneven stitches, and stranding too tightly will cause the knitting to pucker.

Most knitters are taught either the 'English' method

where the yarn is held in the right hand, or the 'Continental' method where the yarn is held in the left hand. Although either method can be used for stranded knitting, the ideal way to work is by using both, i.e. knitting with a yarn in each hand. By doing this you will avoid having to drop one colour to pick up the second. The right-hand yarn always crosses over the left-hand yarn, and the left-hand yarn always crosses underneath the right-hand yarn (see next page). This means that the two yarns will never twist together and become entangled. Indeed, if you work with one hand only, twisting the yarns can be avoided if you consistently cross one colour over and the other colour under.

If there is a stretch of more than seven stitches in one colour, it is advisable to weave in the yarn at the centre of the stretch to avoid a long loose strand of yarn.

STEEKS

Steek is the common term used to describe the extra stitches which are worked at openings, in order that knitting may proceed in the round. In the Fair Isle designs in this book there are 10 extra stitches worked at all openings. The beginning of the round is always placed at the centre of the first steek to be worked.

On a pullover, the beginning of the round is placed at the centre of the first underarm and then at the centre of the first armhole steek. This means that when the steek is cut open up the centre, all the yarn ends joined in and broken off at the beginning

stranding yarn using right-hand yarn

stranding yarn using left-hand yarn

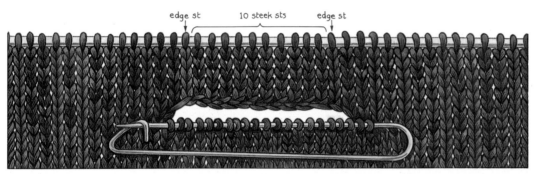

edge st | 10 steek sts | edge st

working a steek

cross stitching a steek

of a round can be trimmed and discarded, thus avoiding the need to darn them in.

On all two-colour rounds, the steek stitches are knit in alternating colours on every stitch and round (above). This helps to lock the yarns within the steek. To ensure that the yarns do not unravel, it is advisable to sew backstitch along the first and last steek stitches before cutting the steek. Do not use a sewing machine as it has a tendency to distort the knitting and forms too rigid a seam. After the backstitch has been completed, use very sharp scissors to cut up the centre of each steek, between the fifth and sixth stitches, so that there will be five steek stitches at each side of the opening. the stitches will not run appreciably. Then the stitches for the sleeves and the neckband can be picked up (just outside the steeks) and the sleeves and neckband can be worked in the round.

Once you have completed the knitting, the steeks must be finished off. To do this, trim the steeks to a two or three stitch width and immediately cross stitch them in position onto the back of the knitting. Begin at the bottom and overcast the steek, catching into the loose strands all the way up (above left). Then work downwards forming cross stitches (above right), not catching the strands, but aiming to cover raw edges.

Edge Stitches

When casting on stitches for a steek, an extra stitch is sometimes cast on, on either side of the steek stitches to form 'edge stitches'. Edge stitches are worked at each side of front openings of cardigans and at dropped shoulder armholes. Front bands and sleeve stitches are picked up from the edge stitch, thus leaving the steek stitches on one side and the patterned stitches on the other. The edge stitch is always worked in the background colour, so that it is easily distinquished from the steek and the patterned stitches.

KNITTING A FAIR ISLE SWATCH

Just as with all designs, it is vital to knit a Fair Isle swatch, in order to determine the correct tension (gauge) before you begin the garment. When Fair Isle patterns are worked in the round (using knit stitches only) they will have a slightly different tension (gauge) than if both knit and purl stitches were used. In this case, it is necessary to knit a swatch in the pattern, using only knit stitches. A circular swatch would have to be very large to give an accurate measurement, and so the best method is to cast on stitches on either a double-pointed or a circular needle. Then work the first row of the chart, and break off the yarns at the end of the row. Slide the stitches to the other end of the needle and work the next row, from the right.

Repeat this process, breaking off the yarns at the end of every row. If you find that the first and last stitches are very loose, just give them a good tug or tie the ends together at the beginning and end of the rows. On completion, gently block and press the knitted swatch, and measure the tension (gauge).

SWISS DARNING

Swiss darning, or duplicate stitch, is embroidery worked on stocking stitch. It is formed by retracing the original knitted stitches, thus overlaying them with a contrasting colour. It is an ideal way of adding small touches of colour, such as on the floral motifs in the ribbings of *Norway* (page 76).

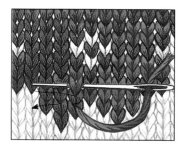

To Swiss darn, thread a tapestry needle with the contrasting yarn and bring it through the work from the back, so that it comes out on the right side at the base of the first stitch to be covered. *Then insert the needle from right to left, under the two threads of the stitch immediately above the stitch to be covered (above). Then take the needle through to the wrong side at the base of the stitch being covered, and bring it to the right side again at the base of the next stitch to be covered (see arrow). Repeat from * until all required stitches are covered.

FINISHING

After the many hours that it takes to complete a knitted garment, do not spoil the finished effect by rushing the final stages. First make sure that all the loose ends of yarn are secured to prevent them unravelling later on. Always leave a long end of yarn for darning in when you start a new ball of yarn. Thread the end into a blunt-ended wool needle and neatly weave it into the back of the knitting behind the stitches of the same colour. Trim the loose end close to the fabric.

Blocking and Pressing
For a perfect fit, the finished pieces of knitting should be blocked to the measurements indicated in the diagrams. This is done before the pieces are sewn together, or, on circular knitting, after the garment has been completed. Blocking can be achieved by using a *woolly board* (see below) or by pinning the pieces out to the required size on a well padded surface and pressing according to the specific yarn label instructions.

For a padded surface, lay a folded blanket on a table and cover it with a sheet. Place the knitted pieces right side down on the sheet and smooth them out to the correct measurements. Check that the fabric is not distorted and that the lines of stitches and rows are straight, then secure to the pad using pins placed at right angles to the edge of the knitting. For most natural fibres, cover the knitting with a damp cloth and, using a warm iron, place it gently onto the fabric and lift it up again – without dragging the iron along the

surface. Allow the knitting to dry completely before removing the pins.

Do not press any areas of ribbing or stitchwork patterns where the cables or other knitted textures can be easily damaged. For a circular Fair Isle garment, press lightly on the wrong side, using a sleeve board for the sleeves.

Backstitch Seam
The most popular seam, the backstitch seam, gives a strong, firm finish to most edges, but forms a ridge on the inside of the garment.

To work the seam, place the pieces to be joined with right sides together, matching any patterns row for row and stitch for stitch. Using a matching yarn, work in backstitch along the seam, close to the edge, sewing into the centre of each row or stitch to correspond with the row or stitch on the opposite edge.

Overcast Seam
Although the overcast seam is worked through two edges placed together, when it is opened out it lies completely flat. Use an overcast seam for areas of ribbing, such as lower borders and cuffs.

With the right sides of the two pieces together and matching stitches and rows, insert the needle behind the knot of the edge stitch on one side, then through the same part of the corresponding stitch on the second side. Draw the yarn through and repeat these actions to join each pair of row ends.

CARE OF HAND KNITTING

The yarns used in this book are made up of natural fibres;

all of them can be hand-washed or dry-cleaned in certain solvents. For further guidance, follow the washing instructions on yarn label.

Hand-washing
For hand-washing, use hand-warm water in which a mild soap has been dissolved. Never allow the garment to soak, or rub it in the water, as the fabric will become felted. Instead, gently squeeze the knitting, supporting it all the time so that the weight of the water does not pull the garment out of shape. Rinse in several changes of water until there is no trace of soap, then spin dry in your washing machine for a short time only.
(**Note:** Read your washing machine instructions very carefully to make sure your machine is suitable for spinning woollens. A sweater should only be spun for a maximum of two minutes and at a maximum speed of 800 rpm.)

Never tumble dry a knitted garment or hang it up to dry. Smooth the garment gently into shape and leave it to dry on a flat surface covered with a towel.

Machine-washing
It is possible to machine-wash some cotton yarns on a gentle cycle, but always refer to the instructions with the yarn.

Woolly Board
The best possible way to finish and subsequently care for your hand knit sweater is to use a woolly board or frame. It dispenses with the need to press the garment and is of particular advantage for textured sweaters which are knitted in the round. There are various types of frames available, but all are made from

wood and are adjustable, so that any size of sweater, from a child to an adult size, can be placed on the frame. (See suppliers on page 127). To finish a newly knitted sweater, rinse the garment and spin (see note on page 124) to remove excess moisture. Remove from the spinner *immediately* and

place on the frame, adjusting to the correct size, and leave to dry away from direct heat. The frame will stretch any ribbing laterally. Remove the garment from the frame when dry and gently steam the ribbing using a kettle and leave to dry flat.

Use the frame to dry your

sweaters after each wash. The great advantages of using a frame are that the garments are shaped to the correct size without the need to use an iron, and raised patterns and cables retain their texture. Also, very importantly, a garment on a woolly board will dry at least twice as quickly as

it would if it were laid flat, because air can circulate inside the garment as well as around the outside. The longer moisture remains in wool, the more it will shrink, therefore using a woolly board will not only assures you of beautifully finished garments, it will also extend their life a great deal.

KNITTING INFORMATION

KNITTING LEVELS
RATING ★ easy knitting
RATING ★★ for average knitters
RATING ★★★ for experienced knitters
RATING ★★★★ challenging knitting

KNITTING ABBREVIATIONS
alt   alternate
approx   approximately
beg   begin(ning)
cm   centimetre(s)
cn   cable needle
cont   continu(e)(ing)
dec   decreas(e)(ing)
g   gram(s)
in   inch(es)
inc   increas(e)(ing)
k   knit
k1b   knit one through back loop
LH   left hand
m   metre(s)

m1   make one st by picking up horizontal loop between sts and knitting into back of it
mm   millimetre(s)
oz   ounce(s)
p   purl
p1b   purl one through back loop
patt(s)   pattern(s)
psso   pass slip stitch over
rem   remain(s)(ing)
rep   repeat(s)(ing)
rev st st   reverse stocking st
RH   right hand
rnd(s)   round(s)
RS   right side(s)
sl   slip
ssk   slip, slip, knit by slipping 2 sts separately knitwise, then insert left-hand needle through front of slipped sts from left and knit them tog
st(s)   stitch(es)
st st   stocking stitch

tbl   through back of loop(s)
tog   together
WS   wrong side(s)
yd   yard(s)
yo   yarn over RH needle to make a new st

KNITTING TERMINOLOGY
U.K.	U.S.A.
cast off	bind off
double knitting yarn	knitting worsted weight yarn
gansey	(fisherman's) sweater
five-ply gansey wool	sport weight wool yarn
four-ply yarn	sport weight yarn
moss stitch	seed stitch
oversew	overcast
slip loop	slip knot
stocking stitch	stockinette stitch
tension	gauge

THE ROWAN STORY

We are proud to announce the publication of *Fishermen's Sweaters* by Alice Starmore. An exciting collection of new patterns by a very talented author, it combines outstanding knitting design with the range and quality of Rowan Yarns.

Rowan is a Yorkshire-based yarn marketing and design company whose name has become synonymous with the revolution that has swept the needlecraft and handknitting industry and changed its image and practice forever. Gone are the limited colours and synthetics offered by most other spinners; we have created a whole knew generation of exciting natural-fibre yarns – from kid silk to chenille – in a myriad colours.

Working with the cream of contemporary designers, including Kaffe Fassett, Edina Ronay and Susan Duckworth, Rowan Yarns commissions special handknitting and needlepoint collections, taking what was once a hobby into the realms of high fashion. Rowan's design collections are now in fashion journals worldwide, while every glossy home supplement bears tasteful evidence of Rowan's artistic craftwork.

Home for Rowan is an old stone mill in a narrow green valley in the shadow of the Pennines overlooking Holmfirth. Rowan Yarns was set up just over thirteen years ago by myself and my colleague Simon Cockin. From the beginning our aims were different from our competitors. We took our palette of yarns to top designers; we worked with them to create yarns in colours to match their specific requirements. Some have proved so popular they have become a permanent part of the Rowan range.

Our yarns are now marketed worldwide and the sheer appeal of the variety and subtlety of colours and textures, combined with our willingness to experiment, ensure our continuing success.

Fishermen's Sweaters sets new standards in quality from one of the very best contemporary designers. The book has been produced with the same care and attention that is given to our yarns and the same eye for form and colour that has been our lifelong hallmark.

We hope that you will enjoy this range of original designs using Rowan's yarns.

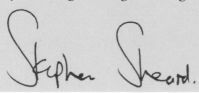

YARN INFORMATION

Most of the sweaters in this book have been worked in various ROWAN yarns. The remaining sweaters have been worked in ALICE STARMORE'S *Scottish Fleet* which is a traditional 5-ply gansey yarn.

It is best to use the yarn specified in the knitting instructions, but if you wish to use a substitute yarn, consult the yarn descriptions given below to find a generic equivalent. (All of the yarns used in the book are standard weights which can be easily matched with other yarn brands.)

Always knit a test swatch with any substitute yarn to make sure that it will achieve the required tension (gauge). If you are unsure about choosing a suitable substitute yarn, ask your yarn shop for assistance.

Important Note: The amount of a substitute yarn needed is determined the number of metres (yards) required rather than by the number of grams (ounces).

YARN DESCRIPTIONS

The following yarns have been used for designs in this book:

Alice Starmore's *Scottish Fleet*
a 5-ply gansey (US sport) weight yarn
100% wool
approx 220m (240yd) per 100g (3½oz) ball

Rowan *Den-m-nit Indigo Dyed Cotton DK*
a medium weight unshrunk cotton yarn
100% cotton
approx 93m (101yd) per 50g (1¾oz) ball

Rowan *Designer DK*
a double knitting (US worsted) weight yarn
100% pure new wool
approx 115m (125yd) per 50g (1¾oz) ball

Rowan *Magpie*
an Aran weight yarn
100% pure new wool
approx 150m (164yd) per 100g (3½oz) hank

Rowan *Silk and Wool*
a 4-ply (US sport) weight yarn
50% mulberry silk/50% superfine botany wool
approx 75m (82yd) per 20g (¾oz) ball

Rowan *Wool and Cotton*
a 4-ply (US sport) weight yarn
50% superfine botany wool/50% Egyptian cotton
approx 150m (164yd) per 50g (1¾oz) ball

ROWAN YARNS ADDRESSES

Rowan yarns can be obtained from stockists of good quality knitting yarns. In case of difficulty in obtaining yarns, write to the addresses below for a list of stockists in your area.

U.K.: Rowan Yarns, Green Lane Mill, Holmfirth, West Yorkshire, England HD7 1RW.
Tel: (0484) 681881

U.S.A.: Westminster Trading Corporation, 5 Northern Boulevard, Amherst, NH 03031.
Tel: (603) 886 5041/5043

Australia: Rowan (Australia), 191 Canterbury Road, Canterbury, Victoria 3126. Tel: (03) 830 1609

Belgium: Hedera, Pleinstraat 68, 3001 Leuven.
Tel: (016) 23 21 89

Canada: Estelle Designs & Sales Ltd, Units 65/67, 2220 Midland Avenue, Scarborough, Ontario M1P 3E6.
Tel: (416) 298 9922

Denmark: Designer Garn, Vesterbro 33 A, DK-9000 Aalborg.
Tel: 98 13 48 24

Finland: Helmi Vuorelma-Oy, Vesijarvenkatu 13, SF-15141 Lahti.
Tel: (018) 826 831

France: Sidel, Ch. Depart. 14C 13840 Rognes.
Tel: (33) 42 50 15 06

Germany: Christoph Fritzsch GmbH, Gewerbepark Dogelmuhle, D-6367 Karben 1.
Tel: 06039 2071

Holland: Henk & Henrietta Beukers, Dorpsstraat 9, NL-5327 AR. Hurwenen.
Tel: 04182 1764

Iceland: Stockurinn, Kjorgardi, Laugavegi 59, ICE-101 Reykjavik.
Tel: (01) 18258

Italy: La Compagnia del Cotone, Via Mazzini 44, I-10123 Torino.
Tel: (011) 87 83 81

Japan: Diakeito Co Ltd, 2-3-11 Senba-Higashi, Minoh City, Osaka 562.
Tel: 0727 27 6604

Mexico: Rebecca Pick Estambresy Tejidos Finos S.A. de C.V., A.V. Michoacan 30-A, Local 3 Esq Av Mexico, Col Hipodromo Condesa 06170, Mexico 11.
Tel: (05) 2 64 84 74

New Zealand: John Q Goldingham Ltd, PO Box 45083, Epuni Railway, Lower Hutt.
Tel: (04) 5674 085

Norway: Eureka, PO Box 357, N-1401 Ski.
Tel: 64 86 55 40

Sweden: Wincent, Sveavagen 94, 113 58 Stockholm.
Tel: (08) 673 70 60

ALICE STARMORE YARN ADDRESSES

Alice Starmore's *Scottish Fleet* yarn (a 5-ply gansey wool) can be obtained in the U.K. and the U.S.A at the addresses below. (See advice above if you wish to purchase a substitute yarn.)

U.K.: Alice Starmore, Isle of Lewis, Scotland.

U.S.A.: Tomato Factory Yarn Co, 8 Church Street, Lambertville, NJ 08530.

WOOLLY BOARD SUPPLIERS

Woolly boards are available in the U.K. and the U.S.A. from the addresses below

U.K.: Jamiesons Knitwear, Commercial Street, Lerwick, Shetland Islands, Scotland.

U.S.A.: Tomato Factory Yarn Company, 8 Church Street, Lambertville, NJ 08530.

ACKNOWLEDGEMENTS

I would like to express my sincere thanks to everyone involved in the making of this book.
To Carey Smith of Anaya Publishers. To my editor, Sally Harding. To Mike Bunn, photographer, and Karen Harrison, stylist. To Clare Clements, book designer, and Windfall Press, chartists. To pattern checker Marilyn Wilson and to knitters Jean Downton, Margaret Finlayson and Peggy Macleod.

SOURCES

Patterns used in my designs Norway, Baltic and Cape Cod are from *Charts for Colour Knitting* by Alice Starmore (publisher: Windfall Press, Isle of Lewis, Scotland).
Patterns used in my design Faroe are from *Føroysk Bindingarmynstur* by Hans M. Debes (publisher: Føroyskt Heimavirki, Tørshavn), and I would like to thank Doreen E. Parkinson for bringing it to my attention.